...andbook.co.uk our purpose is to uncove , muse, debate and celebrate micro-aspects of the tastes and behaviours of the modern middle classes, across endless subjects from motoring to food and drink. We bring tips to soothe worries, give a heads-up on brands to watch, inspire talking points, identify trends, provide the inside track on stuff MCs need to know and, when necessary, settle questions of etiquette.

The Middle Class Handbook – devised by creative practice Not Actual Size – started life in 2009 as a blog dedicated to exploring the stuff modern British middle classes say, do, think and buy. Since then, it has grown into a vibrant hub for all things middle class, spawning published books, a buzzing online network, one-off events, flagrantly middle-class merchandise, and a specialist MC brand consultancy. And as it has grown, so has the range of contributors behind the daily blogs, ranging from teachers and estate agents, to farmers and IT support workers.

www.middleclasshandbook.co.uk
Twitter @MiddleClassHB
Devised by Not Actual Size

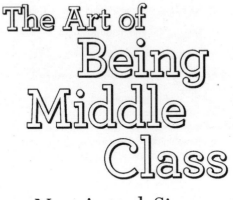

The Art of Being Middle Class

Not Actual Size

Constable • London

CONSTABLE

First published in Great Britain in 2012 by Constable,
an imprint of Constable & Robinson Ltd.

This paperback edition first published in 2016 by Constable

A CIP catalogue record for this book
is available from the British Library.

ISBN: 978-1-4721-2477-7

Printed in Great Britain by Clays Ltd, St Ives plc

Papers used by Constable are from well-managed forests
and other responsible sources.

MIX
Paper from
responsible sources
FSC® C104740

Constable
is an imprint of
Little, Brown Book Group
Carmelite House
50 Victoria Embankment
London EC4Y 0DZ

An Hachette UK Company
www.hachette.co.uk

www.littlebrown.co.uk

Contents

Introduction

What does it mean to be middle class? What do modern British MC people say, do and buy, and why? This is the question pondered by The Middle Class Handbook every day – and through all our field work and observation there is one sensibility that has emerged as a binding force. Awkwardness. It governs every little moment in middle-class life – every thought, action and interaction. To be MC is to hesitate and dither at every turn, consumed by the fear of potential embarrassment and social catastrophe. And that's what this book is all about.

In these pages, middle-class readers should consider their foibles and tribulations understood and celebrated. There's no such thing as 'too middle class' or 'so bloody middle class' – accusations that may well have been levelled at you from time to time. 'Bloody MC' is a great way to be. Those of us who live in a perpetual state of awkwardness and self-doubt have a heightened awareness of how our actions affect everybody around us. We're desperately worried about causing offence and appearing rude. And that's lovely, isn't it? More people could stand to be a bit more bloody MC, really.

But being so wrapped up in improving the overall impression we have on our social circle can be exhausting – going on the right sort of holiday, having just the right sort of cooker hood, pushing the appropriate buggy, etc., because we still live in a nation and culture riddled with class snobbery. But the focus has shifted from background, education, accent and profession to questions of taste. In particular, taste as defined through consumer choice; even more specifically, taste as defined through brand loyalties. And all this pride and anxiety about 'stuff' and what it says about you can make you lose your way.

The average MC person lives in a constant state of insecurity – feeling nervous, unsure of their tastes, preoccupations, behaviours and sensibilities. We not only understand these sensibilities; we think they're brilliant, sometimes funny and something to be proud of. So this book is here to recognise the conceits that make middle-class life quite such a tense, worrisome business, and to offer tips and advice to help you say, do and buy all the right things.

What on earth do you do when someone's bag is taking up a whole seat on a busy train and you want to sit down? What's the correct way to approach the communal cheese board at a dinner party? What can be done about guests who stay a bit too long after dinner? What are the top five places to locate your Sky dish to make sure people can't see you have one? How do you subtly boast about your summer holiday destination? What are the best twee understatements that will cover up your indulgent behaviour ('enjoying a slice of cake' when you're actually scoffing a whole chocolate gateau)? Why is it quite so important to our self-image that we keep making an effort with Chekhov, muesli, Westerns and that Stalingrad book despite them all being utterly tedious? Why on earth do we hide our pants?

Do. Not. Panic. We have all the answers to these and many, many more questions. This book observes, champions and chivvies along Britain's worried twenty-first century middle classes as you navigate umpteen awkward everyday moments and dilemmas. It's a handbook of taste and etiquette, a conspiratorial cheer and a kick up the bum when necessary.

Reading this book will help you master of the art of being middle class. We're not saying it will rid you of your hang-ups – we would hate to do that, because there's no such thing as 'too middle class', remember. But, it will draw your attention to them so you know why you're doing what you're doing, and you can refine your methods for ultimate effect. This book is here to understand and soothe, and to help you, our marvellous British MCs, be the best you can be.

No longer will you sigh and cringe about your middle-classness. You're MC, and we've got your back.

Chapter 1

How to Eat

The middle-class relationship with food and drink is loaded with awkwardness and anxiety. Why do squeezy plastic bottles of pickle and mustard make us feel not just awkward but actually a bit *humiliated*? Why is real gravy a status symbol at the middle-class lunch? Why should we never give up on muesli, resigning ourselves to eternal breakfast cereal disappointment? Is it OK to make sex noises while you eat? (Definitely not.) Follow us as we analyse this relationship and provide a clear, calm and collected guide to some big middle-class food dilemmas. We'll start in the only right and proper place, which happens to be fraught with tensions: the cheeseboard.

An Essential Guide to Cheeseboard Etiquette

How did such a humble foodstuff as cheese become a minefield of social etiquette? Marital rifts open up at dinner parties because the husband has cut the nose off the Brie; people send the cheese course back in a restaurant because it hasn't sufficiently 'breathed'; you have to scrape bits of runny cheese off the hard one because someone has used the wrong knife; people are overheard asking whether they are supposed to eat the rind of the Yarg. And we have still not reached a consensus as to whether the cheese course should come before or after the dessert. Or rather, 'pudding'.

Most cheese, like most red wine, should be served at room temperature, not fridge temperature, in order that their flavours can be appreciated to the full (obviously this rule does not apply to cream cheese or fondue). Ideally the cheeses should be arranged from mildest to strongest, although most people go with whatever looks pretty.

The game of helping yourself to the cheeseboard is to try to keep each cheese intact, if at all possible. This is easy if you have a long log or wheel-shaped bit of cheese, but a 3D mathematical challenge when it comes to pyramids and wedges. On no account lift an entire cheese from the board onto your plate; they are not fairy cakes.

It's also important that everyone gets to taste both the best bit of the cheese and the worst – hence no nicking the nose of the Brie – and that

everyone takes a bit of the rind. Whether or not you choose to eat the rind depends on what the rind's made of and how much of a gastro show-off you want to be.

If you're doing Atkins, or just don't care for water biscuits, cheese on its own, lifted to the mouth with a fork, is encouraged. But take care to follow everyone else in using the same knife for the same cheese – no one wants Stinking Bishop on their Tomme de Montagne (and that's not a euphemism), or bits of goat's cheese in the membrillo.

How to Behave in a Gastro Pub

Gastro pubs were conceived in the nineties to take the old uptightness and formal rituals out of eating good food. The middle classes, however, find it hard to take formal rituals and uptightness out of anything without replacing them with some new etiquette. In truth, gastro pubs are now as riddled with unspoken rules as a Pall Mall club. Here are the ten most important.

1 Finish your pint before starting the food

If you're midway through a pint when the food and wine arrive, do you finish the beer before starting the wine, leave it, or drink both together? The situation is best dealt with by holding back ordering a pint at all. If you can't resist, you should deftly and inconspicuously sink it as the food arrives.

2 Do adjust the table

Gastro pub tables are always, always uneven, and the chance of someone getting up, tilting the table violently and spilling a drink is high. Kudos awaits the person who confidently doubles up a beermat and jams it under the offending table leg.

3 Don't order ostentatious omissions

Competitively healthy people sometimes try to trump those ordering the least calorific dish by requesting a modification that would make it even less fattening (salad instead of chips, no dressing on the salad and so on). This is unacceptable; it creates a terrible atmosphere.

4 Be careful who you share food with

If two people who know each other well are eating together, no one will object if both take a sample forkful of their dish and place it on the edge of their fellow diner's plate so that they can try it. When there are more than four people, this is rather more awkward, but it can be acceptable – even endearing – if one diner makes a particular request for 'a try' of someone else's. On no account should 'a try' be forked or spooned directly into someone else's mouth. This is vulgar and should only happen behind closed doors between people who are in a relationship.

5 Do not have a mass fag break

If some smokers in the party decide to go outside for a cigarette, that's fine, but it is unacceptable

to leave one person on their own, and not ideal to leave two; in the latter case, they will almost certainly bitch about you.

6 If you must order dessert, share it

Middle-class diners have become uncomfortable with dessert, as eating a whole one is seen as unhealthy and a bit greedy. It is, though, acceptable to share one. A sharing partner can be identified by tentatively asking if anyone is having dessert. A potentially interested dessert-sharer might then say, 'I was thinking about it . . .', whereupon you should say, 'Well, do you want to share one?' If no sharer comes forward, but someone urges you to 'have one if you like', you can say you were just interested in finding out what the odd-sounding dessert on the menu looked like, and then change the subject.

7 Be bold in dealing with the last bit

The problem with sharing dessert – and other shareable dishes such as potato skins or garlic bread – is that you will probably be left with a last bit, which everyone feels too self-conscious to take.

Our recommended simple solution is to ask, 'Does anyone else want this?' and when no one says, 'Yes', boldly and confidently eat it. Everyone else will feel grateful to you for dispelling the awkwardness. If you want to avoid this situation but still share a dessert, try the cheese, which is easier as it comes in several distinct 'parts'. In this case, don't forget to . . .

8 Discuss the cheese

Middle-class people hugely enjoy talking about the provenance of things, especially food. As modern cheese plates usually come with a guide to their origin, other diners will appreciate a few minutes' debate on the subject ('I never knew there was a Northamptonshire cheese! How interesting!' and so forth).

9 Pay with a card

These days, everyone knows that it's bad form to ask for a reduction in your contribution to the bill because you didn't have dessert/wine/ whatever, although if other diners suggest it, it is OK to accept this. To split the bill, everyone should hand over cards and ask the waiter to take an equal share from each. Don't produce cash, as this will lead to confusion, with someone taking your cash, paying for both on the card and disorientating the waiter.

10 Tip as per a restaurant

Customers in gastro pubs tend to tip far smaller amounts than they do in restaurants. This is mean, irritating to staff and unjustified; if anything, gastro staff will be paid less than their restaurant counterparts.

How Middle Class is your Pub?

The pub snack has long been an important part of going out for a drink. Maybe it's because you fancy something nice and salty to accompany your bottle of Belgian beer. Maybe it's because you want to bond with someone over some interesting nuts. Or maybe it's because you went straight to the pub after work without having any tea and by half past nine, the five pints of Staropramen on an empty stomach mean that you need to eat three packets of crisps in quick succession to stop you keeling over.

A few years ago, these snacks began to go upmarket.

First, as we all remember, came the posh crisp. The crisps themselves became chunky and irregular, and the flavours moved up several notches in class terms. Cheese and onion became sour cream and chive; salt and vinegar became balsamic vinegar with crushed sea salt; ready salted was replaced with cracked black pepper and so on. More recently there's been another, major change in the type of bar snacks pubs sell. You might have heard, 'Oh, sorry, we don't sell them any more. We do tapas now instead.'

But tapas don't serve the same purpose as a packet of crisps. You can hardly share bowls of second-rate patatas bravas, grilled halloumi or calamari rings in the same way as you can a few packets of Walkers salt and vinegar. This is an extreme case, of course, but an increasing number of pubs no longer sell simple bar snacks. You know the ones – the nice salty little snacks that you can eat from the packet without fuss or mess. Increasingly, middle-class pubs sell exotic nibbles and bowls of outlandishly flavoured nuts, seeds, straw, worms or whatever.

So, is your pub middle class? Just check out the snacks it sells. Here's a handy guide:

ORDINARY PUB	MIDDLE-CLASS PUB
Nobby's chilli nuts	Bowl of chilli puffs
KP dry roasted peanuts	Wasabi peas
Walkers grab bag	Burts chips
Doritos	Nachos sharing platter
Bombay mix	Japanese rice crackers
Salted peanuts	Toasted cashews
Bags of cockles	Moules marinières*
Mr Porky pork scratching	Artisanal pork scratchings
*only available in the dining area, of course	

NB Pickled eggs, like dimpled pint glasses, can currently be found both in old-school ordinary pubs and fashionable middle-class ones reviving traditional English food. There are some other snack foods, a no-man's-land sub-genre, that can be found in both. These aspire to middle-classness, but seem really not to know what they are or who they're for: Twiglets, Mini Cheddars, Scampi Fries and perhaps even McCoy's crisps.

Real Gravy: the Dinner-Party Weapon

Back in the seventies and eighties, there was something very naff about the whole idea of gravy. It was acceptable with Sunday lunch, but apart from that it smacked of the olde-worlde, insular postwar British cooking that smart young things were rejecting with their sauces and dishes from Italy, France, China and India.

Liking gravy signified parochial Little-Englander-dom; after all, the inauthentic chicken tikka masala had supposedly been created to satisfy drunk Englishmen demanding some gravy with their delicately spiced wonder from the subcontinent. Little wonder gravy became so devalued that no educated person under forty could (or wanted to) make it, and for most people who did want it, its creation began with Bisto's plant-food-resembling instant granules.

Of course the middle classes did still eat real gravy, but to escape embarrassment, it had to be rebranded as 'jus'.

It is, surely, thanks to the revival of interest in traditional British cooking that the word and concept of 'gravy' has regained respectability, but the problem is that now barely anyone knows how to make it, and these days instant granules are simply un-acceptable at the middle-class table.

The ability to cook your own gravy for

a joint of organic beef or comfort sausage and mash has become a middle-class status symbol, a sign that you can cook without recipe books, and we advise you to teach yourself, immediately. Plonk down the boat with self-conscious casualness and show off your gravy literacy. And when someone asks you how you make it, say, 'Oh, just chuck some mustard and cornflour in the roasting pan', as if it's *de rien*, while you enjoy the meaty pride bubbling up inside you.

Muesli: the Eternal Disappointment

There's just no really nice brand of muesli, is there? We try to eat it because it's healthy, and we alternate brands because we keep thinking that *this time* we have found the right one. Alpen is too sugary and powdery; no-sugar Alpen is just powdery; Waitrose own-brand is like pet food; Jordans has just enough nuts and oats to feel like punishment. We did think that Dorset Cereals, despite that babyish copywriting on the box – why do all brands feel they have to talk to you like a chummy primary-school teacher? – had the answer, but you soon get sick of there being too many big 'Chilean flame' raisins and the fake-fruit-flavoured oats. (When did we reach the point where simple raisins had to be 'Chilean flame'?) The only course of action is simply to accept that muesli is tedious – but persist with it, because it's a middle-class cornerstone. For extra virtuous misery points, mix your own original muesli invented by Maximilian Bircher-Benner: mix together some soaked oats, some almonds or hazelnuts, grated fresh apple and lemon juice.

Trying Without Buying at Food Markets

The middle-class vogue for street food has reached the point where some places are holding mini 'food festivals' which turn out to be rows of stalls selling stand-up snacks from around the world. This is a very pleasant and welcome trend, of course, especially if you like paella and empanadas, but these places are extremely nerve-jangling for the middle classes.

How do you try the tasty and appetising samples without a) worrying you look like a pig, and b) feeling as if you've entered into a contract that will be impossible to break? The upper classes hoover up the samples like it's a buffet, tend to talk loudly while doing so, then move on. Similarly, the working

classes see it for what it is: a marketing exercise designed to sell and happily enjoy a sample then carry on purchasing whatever they were looking for. Meanwhile, the poor old MCs are in a quandary, wracked with worry about taking more than one sample of condiment on a cracker and beginning a process that can only lead to buying something you don't want for fear of seeming greedy and rude. What you need is a few stock phrases to help you walk away having tried but decided not to buy. Here are three you should have up your sleeve:

'Oh, how delicious. I wish I didn't already have the

cheese breathing at home for tonight. I'll definitely come back for some of this next time.'

'It's so tempting to buy some, but I'm watching my BMI and you know how it is, a moment on the lips . . .'

'I'm going to carry on looking round but stay right where you are, I'll be back to pick some of this up before I leave.'

Please Just Stop: Sex Noises while Eating

A note to those people who find it necessary to make orgasm noises while sampling food. Taking the first mouthful of a rare-breed steak in a crowded restaurant is not actually the same thing as having sex. Nor is sampling a sliver of really runny Brie in a specialist cheese shop.

Therefore it is not appropriate to make those groaning sex noises while eating these things. Especially not in a public place. Like a shop. Or a restaurant.

You might think it makes you look like a cultured foodie whose senses are so finely tuned that the merest whiff of quality sends you into spasms of delight. Someone so high-minded that they can find the same depth of pure pleasure in culture that more base humans can only find in sex. In fact, it just makes you look like you aren't getting any.

No one wants to hear your sex noises, especially not when they too are eating, which is one of the many reasons why actual sex in public places is also frowned upon.

Squeezy Condiment Bottles: Awkward

Ketchup has long been offered in a squeezy plastic alternative to the standard glass condiment bottle, but we're seeing all sorts of products following suit, whether it's sensible or not, and this is something that makes the MCs very uncomfortable: Marmite, mustard, jam, honey, salad cream, mango chutney, pickle. They all come in squeezy bottles these days. If you're satisfied with 'smooth', 'no bits' and 'small chunk' versions of everything, you needn't buy another glass-bottled condiment for the rest of your days.

But all this squeezing is really awkward at the table, and the middle-class person finds it actually kind of humiliating when someone squirts out the English mustard and it forms an unfortunate yellow pile on the plate, or when the Branston bottle's nearly empty and someone starts noisily pumping out air with the pickle. This won't do. Simple, polite, quiet, glass condiment bottles are always preferable in middle-class homes.

Ostentatious Refusal of the Children's Menu

A new snobbery has taken over restaurants: the ostentatious refusal of the children's menu. Large mixed family parties and nuclear families of four are favouring the more mature menu for their kiddiewinks. The mothers usually make all the decisions, however, as their husbands sit there trying to go unnoticed, flushing scarlet. But you can almost read their minds: 'Just give him some bloody baked beans if that's what he wants!' Many a middle-class mother has hissed something like, 'Darling, you'll like it – I promise. It's just like you had the other day.' Unfortunately, and this becomes obvious as the waitress clears away half a pound of artichokes on a plate, this isn't true.

While the 'five-a-day' boom of the noughties, or even Jamie O's school dinners' spruce-up, may have something to do with this craze, it seems the main snobbery over the children's menu is far simpler. The middle classes like to project the image that our child has a finer palate than anyone else's, which they will eagerly build upon, the more trips out to restaurants they take.

Look here. This needs to stop. Children have their whole lives to acquire the taste for olives and capers. There's no harm in letting your kids eat from the children's menu once in a while. Adults can go to a restaurant and sink five bottles of Pinot Grigio, but kids can't have the odd plate of Alphabetti Spaghetti? Has the world gone mad?

Chapter 2

The Right and Proper Way to Dress

The middle classes do not tend to lead the way in matters of style. It all moves a bit too quickly for us, and working out what to wear and how to wear it is a persistent worry, sometimes an irritation. How is it that trainers are the source of such bewilderment and self-doubt? Is there a right and a wrong way to wear sunglasses in April? When's the right time of year for a woman to start wearing tights again? Why is it that wealthier men just don't know how to wear jeans? This chapter explains and soothes these wardrobe worries. We'll start with a pretty central middle-class quandary:

How to Wear Sunnies in April Without Looking Like a Twat

On a sunny day when it's still nippy out, do you wear sunglasses and risk looking like a pretentious,

vain wannabe pretending they don't want to be recog-
nised, or risk frying your retinas? Our brief and totally
unscientific research in one of south London's bourgeois
enclaves produced the following rules:

- *Sitting at a pavement table outside a cafe* Yes. Almost
  compulsory, we'd say. Makes you look at ease
  with your cosmopolitan lifestyle. Accessorise with
  small dog.
- *Walking down the street (sunny side)* OK, as long as
  the street is consistently sunny, not ducking in
  and out of shade. Sunnies must be removed when
  stopping to greet a friend.
- *Walking down the street (shady side)* No. And not on
  top of head, either. Tuck into pocket or cross the
  road.
- *With Bermuda shorts and deck shoes, or a strappy dress*
  No. For God's sake, it's only April.
- *With coat (preferably puffa jacket) and scarf* Good
  for working a sort of après-ski or Rome-in-
  January look.
- *Oversized quiff, fifties dress, or other retro styling* Yes,
  as long as glasses match period of styling.
- *Big sunglasses with conspicuous logo (Chanel, Dior, Gucci)*

Can be worn in any situation, indoors or out, at any time of year providing you are a rich expat or don't mind being mistaken for one.

- *On the school run* Only if you drive a people mover or a Mini – probably to an independent prep school – or if you don't mind people thinking you do.

When to Pull up your Waistband

Twenty-four years old is the cut-off for a man to get away with a low-slung waistband. Why so young? Why so cruelly specific? Well, the whole concept of an unruly waistband playing a precarious game of frottage with one's crotch and lower-arse area came out of US gang culture. Gang members would get arrested in their baggy jeans and have their belts and their shoelaces confiscated to stop them attempting suicide by hanging. Consequently baggy denim trews would hang low and tough, showing off lots of underpant elastic. Shoes showed lots of tongue. A look was born. And it's rather embarrassing if, by twenty-four, a self-respecting British middle-class man hasn't got over his morbid, comic-book fascination with this.

Beyond twenty-four, the MC man can carry on liking rap music, still nod his head to a Jay-Z or Kanye tune at a wedding, but once he starts working for a living and finds a cut of suit (with proper trousers) that flatters him, trying to relate to slackers, surfers, moshers and skateboarders via some sort of mystical waistband semaphore becomes a bit, well . . . embarrassing.

You don't have to go Clarkson or Cowell with your pants once you hit your quarter-century. Just find a cut of trouser that actually fits properly, sits on your hips nicely, doesn't infantilise your body, isn't endorsed by the guys from JLS, doesn't inspire you to break out into a chorus of 'Pretty Fly for a White Guy' when you look in the mirror, and doesn't require a sideways-skewed baseball cap to set it off. Ditto skinny jeans.

How to React to a Gift of Jewellery When You're Already Bejewelled

There's a very awkward moment for the MC woman to negotiate when she receives a gift of jewellery and she's already wearing some. Does she immediately put the new piece on and keep it on for the rest of the evening, even if it clashes horribly with her outfit and/or other jewellery? If she doesn't try it on at all, she risks offending the person who gave it to her. What on earth does she do if she receives *two or more* pieces of jewellery on the same occasion? We have devised a four-step strategy to help you navigate this tense situation should it happen to you:

1 When getting ready for an occasion that might involve being given presents, anticipate jewellery gifts. Don't choose statement jewellery; pick something you would be happy to take off later if necessary.

2 Immediately put on the new jewellery. The jewellery-giver will always say, 'No, don't worry, you don't have to wear it now.' If the new item is a perfect match with your outfit, say, 'I've actually been desperate for the right jewellery for this outfit.'

3 If the item clashes, it's definitely acceptable not to wear it for the whole evening. Say, 'I adore it, and I have just the thing to wear it with. I'll wear it next time I see you.'

4 If you are given two or more jewellery gifts, try each of them on, then put them back in their boxes/wrapping. Say that you'll give each one a proper outing another time.

How to Wear a Hoody

If you're over forty and contemplating wearing a hoody, the key thing to bear in mind is that oversized garments on middle-aged, middle-class people are always totally unacceptable.

Therefore, your hoody should have a distinctly un-hip hop, un-teenage snug fit. That way, you can look benign and cosy and steer clear of any of those scary and threatening connotations.

Ideally, the hood itself should not go up, so that you avoid adopting the sinister and intimidating 'cobra' stance that gives pensioners and corner-shop owners the collywobbles. Don't do that weird thing of going all off-duty-Vegas-legend with them – a pristine white Versace hoody with gold diamante details is very ageing . . . or very Peter Andre, depending on how you look at it.

Ladies: When to Start Wearing Tights Again

Few would disagree that there is something unsightly and, let us be frank, common about the sight of a pallid leg in the depths of January, and even something a little desperate about one slathered in fake tan in November. But the question is, at what point does this distastefulness set in? A honeyed natural tan on a fine day in October is surely OK, but a black tight on a chilly day in August looks a little, well, elderly. So when exactly during the autumn or winter should a middle-class lady dig some tights out of her drawer and begin wearing them in public again? Our guideline for today's middle-class girl about town is that the middle two weeks in September are the safest time, with an option of pushing into mid-October *if* you have good legs and a deep, *natural* tan.

Neck Uncertainty and the Vexed Issue of Tie-Wearing in the Post-Casual World of Work

Neckwear has become something of an issue in business. It is almost impossible to guess whether any European client will be wearing one (in other countries, especially warmer ones, ties are less common, and less socially charged). And it matters, because if one of you is and the other isn't, the meeting tends to feel awkward at first. Indeed, the misunderstandings can affect the business you do.

The MC man was happier pre-nineties, before open-necked shirts and chinos became acceptable, and dress-down Fridays became de rigueur in some of the trendier offices. Why? Because back then, when everyone dressed in that uptight and boring style, you knew where you were and what to wear. Preparing for a meeting with a new client who was going to bring along a few colleagues, it was easy: grey suit, white shirt, black shoes, plain blue tie – done. You'd all turn up looking more or less the same, not take any notice of each other's clothes and crack on with the conversation.

Nowadays, however, with any client who you feel might be just slightly with-it, you have neck uncertainty. You might turn up in a tie to find them not wearing ties, in which case you feel ill at ease and very much as if you're trying to sell something, rather than having a conversation. Vice versa, and you feel as if you haven't shown the company enough respect.

All you can do, really, is take comfort from the fact that you're not alone in your uncertainty. All

MC men have neck uncertainty; nobody is quite sure who's leading the way, and they live in hope that the popularity of *Mad Men* will bring back formal styles.

The Nine Pairs of Shoes that Ought to be Enough for Any Middle-Class Woman

The MC woman used to have an ambivalent relationship with fashion. She was willing to keep up with it, not wishing to appear frumpy, but was very much inclined towards 'classics' rather than 'hot new trends'. Over the last ten years or so, however, that has changed. Some ascribe this to *Sex and the City*, but cause and effect is rarely so clear-cut; one has to ask why *SATC* attracted such a large audience in the first place.

Anyway, the upshot of this is that while the MC woman's wardrobe was once fairly basic, unchanging and essentially an evolved version of her mother's, these days it is a little more trend-based and shifting. Take the shoes. When once she could pretty much have done it all in court, loafer and sandal, she now packs more options (even a sport shoe worn for leisure!) and these can change from year to . . . Well, let's say half-decade to half-decade. Those wishing to fit in will need the following:

1 Ballet pump, ideally French Sole
Possibly her favourite shoe; it secretly reminds her of being younger and going to ballet class. For off-duty days, really; so easy and perfect for the awkward winter–spring transition when she's still wearing tights but boots seem too much.

2 Low-heeled slingback
For dressing up, especially for work parties. Might also have stilettos, but hardly ever wears them. Zara acceptable these days, but preferably L.K.Bennett or Russell & Bromley.

3 Loafer
Doesn't have to be the v. expensive Tod's, but that's where she's aiming. Perfect for light duty-wear: possibly the office, school parents' evenings, visiting parents.

4 Havaianas
A hangover from holidays, and the MC-liberating embrace of boho – one of the early Big Trends she bought into in the noughties.

5 Converse All-Star

In plain white. Modern Adidas and Nike trainers are still a little de trop. Good for Sunday afternoon city strolls and pub lunches.

6 Wellington boot

For the country and snow. Not necessarily in green – that's an old-fashioned joke from the days when there were fewer colours. The posher country set is likely to go for plain Hunter; the more adventurous welly-wearer will go for Liberty-style patterns and fun colours.

7 Brogue

True, they make your feet look big, but then the nice middle-class girl always does look a bit big in the foot. (It fits, somehow, suggesting country pursuits.) The brand doesn't matter, but there are nice ones in Office and Clarks.

8 Shoe boot

Probably suede. Middle-class women don't like to teeter, so they will shy away from shoe boots with stiletto heels and opt for the chunkier, more sensible sort. Clarks and Aldo have the answer.

9 Mary Jane

In fun colours. She likes these because, a bit like the ballet pumps, there's a schoolgirlish quality to them. And she can tolerate them quite high; they're actually really comfortable because of the ankle strap.

Footwear: Everything a Man Needs to Know

Although there can be some grey areas between middle and other classes when it comes to clothing (where exactly do we stand on Barbour these days, for example? Or even Polo Ralph Lauren?), it is still possible to tell a middle-class man from his shoes.

The rule is simple. The true working-class male never owns (discounting trainers) more than four pairs of shoes; his middle-class counterpart owns at least five. These are:

• Two pairs of black leather shoes, one with laces, mostly worn for work between Monday and Thursday.
• One pair of brown or oxblood lace-ups, worn for

work on Fridays. These black and brown work shoes are very likely to be made by Church or Oliver Sweeney.

- Two pairs of casual shoes, most likely including a pair of loafers and/or a pair of Clarks.
- A pair of walking boots, important for walking at weekends and/or on holiday.

The MC male may well own a pair of rugged Merrell shoes in addition to the walking boots. He will also

have a pair of Argyll wellies, of course. On top of these he may also add brogues, deck shoes, Chelsea boots or any one of a great variety of footwear; the point is, he will never have fewer than five on the go at any one time. The question of trainers outside of the gym has been known to be very problematic . . .

The Trouble with Trainers

Deep down, the middle classes are slightly embarrassed by the 'box fresh' trainers so beloved of the working classes. We feel very self-conscious in shiny new white sneakers because it has been drummed into us that newness in clothes, shoes and furniture is a bit . . . naff.

During his schooldays, the middle-class chap is not allowed to be a slave to trends with his choice of sneaker. He gets one pair and makes 'em last. For MC males, the idea that a pair of barely worn, perfectly presentable running shoes must be discarded because they aren't cool any more is not a concept that is encouraged by their penny-pinching parents. Ergo, what trainers MC types do get to own – sometimes for many years – take on a sentimental significance.

When it comes to buying a new pair in adult life, the

MC man's choice is governed by his heart and by his innate sense of parsimony. Just as Dad sticks with the same style of brogue he's had since early adulthood, the average MC trainer-shopper is looking for longevity, not fashionableness. He wants to invest in a heritage brand, an old-school design, a tried-and-tested classic.

But, as sportswear has become ubiquitous, there are now sporty shoes that middle-class men don't really think of as trainers but as a more stylish option because they are not chunky and brightly coloured. The top five you can consider acceptable as a MC man are:

- All vintage-looking gym shoes
- Prada sport trainers
- Camper Pelotas, which are still kicking about
- Converse All-Star
- Vans Chukka Boots

Style on the Slopes

For some middle-class women, skiing is an opportunity to show off their style as much as their freestyle. There are a few key tribes you need to be aware of when next navigating the pistes. And ladies, maybe you recognise yourself in one of our tribes. Are you Shouty Chalet Girl Charlotte, whose sartorial ski icon is the sturdy, no-nonsense Kate Middleton? Or maybe you're a Mo-Girl, adhering to the strict, three-garment thermal/fleece/windproof system? Read on to find out.

Heidi High Street

It's middle-of-the road Heidi High Street's first time on the slopes, and she's not so sure. Will she get a headache/vertigo/a nosebleed up there? Do they have Starbucks, Monsoon and Jigsaw in the Alps? She certainly isn't prepared to take a risk and invest in any expensive kit, so some cheap and cheerful improvising using wintry-ish stuff from her existing, urban wardrobe will have to do: a puffa from Uniqlo, a fleece from Gap, snowboardy ski pants from TK Maxx, gloves from H&M. Result? She feels poor and unfashionable next to the Siberian Russkis and Dollygarchs. Slow, ungainly and silly watching all the superfast Shouty Charlottes and Mo-Girls from the blue runs and nursery slopes. And, worst of all, *really bloody cold*. Heidi High Street will be back in St Lucia next winter.

The Siberian Russki

The hatchet-faced billionaire Dollygarch loves skiing. Our unsmiling Siberian Russki doesn't do boring stuff like practicality, flexibility and insulation, aspiring to look like an expensive Alpine call girl and favouring the Darth-Vader-in-the-Dolomites Chanel outfits (in leather!) as worn by that wonderful attention-seeking Victoria Beckham. (That's including Chanel skis, costing a barmy £1,325 – four times the price of pro skis for ten times the naffness.)

Like her winter fashion icons Paris Hilton and Ivanka Trump, our turbo Russki skis only the pistes

immediately adjacent to the upmarket resort centre (Courchevel and St Moritz, mostly), worried about the lack of sushi bars, photographers and plastic surgeons if she ventures above the treeline. She is not the natural winter-sports type. Her hair extensions freeze to the inside of her fur hat, her great big, non-sports-specific Dior sunglasses remain welded to her face – she resembles a Touche Éclat'd panda if she takes them off – and the temperature freezes up the Botox in her forehead. Which, at least, negates the need for a crash helmet.

Shouty Chalet Girl Charlotte

Sturdy girls like Sloaney Charl colonise the rowdier Alpine resorts (Val D'Isère, Méribel, Zermatt) with their braying, boozing, boy-chasing and bad clothes. They aren't trying to be fashionable, pursuing instead a blue-blooded, 'born-to-it' insouciance.

Mismatched clobber in primary colours from any of the Fulham Road-based ski outfits (White Stuff, Fat Face) is appropriated from the chalet company's lost-property box, pilfered off boyfriends or blagged from visiting gear reps and teamed with the odd, intentionally contrapuntal accessory – a Kensington school sweatshirt, say – a mujahideen scarf or a tweed cap. Her sartorial ski icon is the equally sturdy and no-nonsense Kate Middleton, but after a few Vodka Red Bulls, Charlotte can start to get all Boujis on the black runs, reverting to Princess Beatrice territory with the perennially unfunny 'Chelsea Yeti' look of silly hat ('hilarious' false dreadlocks protruding from a woolly rasta hat, anyone?) and a daft, Wookie-inspired fleece. Deep down she thinks boys who ski in shorts or dinner jackets are a *rairly bloody good laugh*, actually. Shouty Chalet Girl Charlotte's natural winter habitat is any branch of Dick's Tea Bar. Drinking the boys under the table, probably.

High Fashionista

Her desire is to be even cooler than the ice cubes in that Yakutsk-temperature cocktail you've just ordered from the outdoor ice bar. That means transferring her brutally discriminating fashionista ways from urban studio pad to vertiginous Chamonix chalet. But while her 'on trend' style makes her look rather groovy, she is also regarded by the sneering, bona fide ski fraternity as the archetypal 'all the gear, no idea' sort. That is to say, there might be Vexed Generation, Stella McCartney for Adidas, bits of Moncler for Balenciaga and/or Watanabe and this season's must-have Ugg earmuffs in her Prada kit bag, but she can't ski for toffee. Hangs out at places like The Clubhouse in Chamonix and the Coco Club in Verbier. Or anywhere she can get five bars of signal strength on her iPhone.

Mo-Girl

Mo-Girls are happiest in among the moguls. Skiing to aggressive Winter Olympiad standards from 9 a.m. until 4.30 p.m., thighs pumping like pistons.

Mo-Girl is more haute route than haute couture and adheres to the strict, three-garment thermal/fleece/windproof system as practised by such adventurous pro labels as Peak Performance, Schoffel, JCC for Rossignol and, if she's feeling extra flush, Arc'teryx or Patagonia (so expensive it's nicknamed 'Patagucci'). Her skis are twin-tipped, four-by-four 'fat boys' by Armada that regularly take her off-piste, so she's avalanche-trained accordingly, carries a collapsible snow shovel in her rucksack, knows how to use a GPS and actually reads the technical jargon on her jacket label. Find her in hardcore Les Gets or Chamonix. She's in bed by 10 p.m., up next day at 8 a.m. Après-ski is for wimps. You Mo-Girl!

The Rules of Male Flesh Exposure

For many middle-class people, shirtlessness equates with chavviness and many pubs ban them along with dirty boots and work clothes. But the new flesh politics involve showing off other areas of the body, in ways that can create, blur and reinforce social boundaries.

Take the low 'V', for example. Truth is, the middle

classes don't like to lead the way with necklines; for decades it was the bromide crew neck that ruled the rugby clubs, estate-agent bars and golfing lounges, covering up shirt acreage and arm flesh with prudish impunity. V-necks were strictly for schoolboys, square older folk and chic Parisian men. So, when the 'he-vage'-exposing V-neck t-shirts – under various casual blazers, coats and leather bombers – came into fashion, the MC males were worried, convinced that they made a man look like a hospital orderly.

And we never liked those weird – and, let's be honest, dead common – high V-neck sweaters with the apex of the V nestling just below the Adam's apple that were de rigueur during the late nineties . . . but gradually the proudly late-adopting middle classes moderated and accepted.

We took a long time, too, to accept the wife-beater vest as anything but M&S-bought underwear to be hidden away beneath shirts and sweaters during the winter months – considering the flaunting of a scoop-neck-vest-as-outerwear to be the trashy preserve of oiks who wanted to show off new tattoos on their flabby biceps. But now, even snooty MC Dad may allow himself to don a simple white vest from M&S when on holiday, toning down its slovenly yobbishness with navy-blue shorts, a Panama hat, a pair of brown leather Sperry Top-Siders and some very much un-inked and scrawny arms.

And have a go at Patio-Heater Casual: a high-street-led look that in the last decade has developed alongside an increasing British fondness for socialising outdoors. It is a mainstream dress code, and one that has spread so gradually that we have not noticed how often it seems to involve exposing skin, nor how much skin is exposed. Get the look: artfully frayed and faded polo shirts, long shorts with sports or military references, cropped trousers, wrap-around shades, sandals or trainers and baseball caps.

Chapter 3

What to Say and How to Say It

Somehow, when middle-class people learned how to communicate, we also learned how to worry enormously and get quite exercised about what every word, pronunciation and inflection conveys. And it's even worse online, where things we commit to a Facebook status update, a tweet or an email can say more about you than you intend. Is there an art to handling social networking the middle-class way? Why the heck do we hold our breath when we check our emails? Why is 'you look tired' quite so

offensive to a middle-class person? Why are 'haitch' and 'boom' totally unacceptable? We'll explore these quandaries here in this guide to MC communication. First up, how to pronounce the word chorizo.

BOOM!

Over-Pronouncing Foreign-Language Words

Exaggerated pronunciation of non-English words is something that distinguishes the MCs, and marks people out along the middle-class spectrum. It starts with basic, fairly accurate and inconspicuous words. When requesting ciabatta, for example, most good middle-class folk make it a point of principle to say the correct 'chuh-*bat*-uh', not 'see-ya-batta' (people saying this makes them ashamed to be British), and almost everyone now says 'Ibeetha' rather than 'Ibitsa', as some did twenty years ago.

But after that there is a scale, with the less showy middle-class people sometimes pronouncing words in ways they know are probably wrong but are unlikely to make them look like show-offs. How many people know chorizo is 'choreetho', but stick with 'choreeso' because the former seems a bit

Hyacinth Bouquet? How many students are aware that Nabokov is properly pronounced Na-*bok*-ov, but feel that *Na*-bo-kov is a safer, more polite bet in Waterstones?

These are the half-steppers, though. For many of those who like their choreethos and Macarrrenyas, there is no limit to their verbal flashiness. When ordering risotto, their role model could be the football commentator Jonathan Pearce doing an Italian game (Rrrroma, Gatoooooo, Pirrrrlohh, and so on); when they mention Calais or Paris they sound

57

like someone from *'Allo 'Allo!* and they might order paella just so they can say 'pay-elyyya'. They know it's Belaroosh not Belarus, Ookraine not Ukraine, and they may even drop, you know, actual foreign words (especially French: jambon, fromage, vin) into everyday speech, with just the minimum of irony.

The point, of course, is to show that you're cosmopolitan, and not an insular British person. Over-pronouncers privately like to think that the vast majority of their fellow Brits are backward-looking Little Englanders, regardless of whether this is true or not. The funny thing is that they think nothing of mispronouncing British place names; if you tried to engage them in a conversation about whether Salford should be Solford or Sallford, or the Newcastle/Ny'cassle issue, they would secretly suspect you of being a member of the BNP.

Should You Say 'Wee', 'Pee' or 'Use the Loo' When Discussing Urination Among Friends?

The word you use for the lavatory/toilet/WC/ restroom/bathroom has been regarded as a signifier of class since Nancy Mitford identified 'lavatory' or 'loo' as upper-class terms in her 1955 essay 'The English Aristocracy'.

Mitford said 'toilet' was a middle and working-class word, but of course things have moved on since then. Not only do we now have 'restroom', 'bathroom' and 'bog', but in recent years there has also been a trend among younger groups of friends to use the childlike 'wee', or the slightly more vulgar 'pee'. Girls in particular will announce to friends in a car that they 'really need a wee' at the next service station; the more unconventional might even use it in a work situation. We would advise against this, generally. The proper MC way is to stick to the old-fashioned-sounding euphemism of 'using' or 'going to' the 'loo'.

'You Look Tired' and Other 'Considerate' Observations

It's astounding to an MC person when somebody says 'you look tired'. What do they hope to achieve by telling you so directly that your state of mind, health or mood is having a negative manifestation on your face? If you happen to look unhappy or unwell, 'Are you all right?' will do nicely, without it then being pointed out *specifically* why you look rubbish. Below are five 'considerate' observations that are most offensive to the well-mannered, sensitive middle classes who simply can't cope with such direct statements:

- 'You look really tired.'
- 'You've gone all red.'
- 'You look shiny.'
- 'You look like you've been crying.'
- 'You really don't look well.'

How to Talk Jafaican, Innit

'As its traditional speakers emigrate to Essex and Hertfordshire, the 650-year-old Cockney accent is dying off in London,' wrote the author Harry Mount in the *Evening Standard*, 'to be replaced by multicultural London English, heavily influenced by West Indian patois, Bangladeshi and remnants of old Cockney.' In other words, to find anyone who talks like Michael Caine you now need to go to Southend-on-Sea, whereas in London, everyone under thirty sounds like the kids from *The Catherine Tate Show*.

Sort of. Mr Mount neglects to mention that this new accent, which he calls 'Jafaican', has also eaten into the posher accents of the middle-class young; you can hear it in Lily Allen's voice and you can certainly hear it from the public schoolboys and girls out in Chelsea on a Saturday night.

For those who are confused, Mount offers a Jafaican glossary; not all of this has been adopted by the posh lot, but among that which has is:

- Buff (attractive)
- Axe (instead of 'ask')
- Skets (derogatory term for loose girls)
- Sick (good)
- Hype (hype things up, increase status)
- Chat (talk back, contradict)
- Innit? (sentence-closer, seeking agreement)

How to Understate your Indulgence

The MCs are very uncomfortable with indulgence. Actually, we have a whole different idea of what counts as indulgence. Many things that would be considered by others as quite normal everyday behaviour are, in the middle-class world, 'treats' or 'letting your hair down'.

We can't just treat and let treat, though; we feel the need to tell other people what we're doing (often on Twitter) because we want to sound totally chilled out about our ability to chill out. But we'll nervously understate, often actually lie, to make our indulgences sound more respectable. Here's what you should say to cover up your indulgences:

WHAT YOU'RE DOING	WHAT TO SAY
Falling asleep reading *Heat* magazine	'Curling up with a good book'
Drinking a whole bottle of Merlot and a little bit from a second bottle	'Enjoying a glass of wine'
Eating most of a chocolate gateau	'Having a slice of cake'
Watching *The X Factor* every weekend and having the hots for Gary Barlow	'I sometimes watch *The X Factor* for a laugh'
Having sex on a Sunday morning	'Lying in and reading the Sunday papers together in bed'

Words Coming Back into Vogue: Crikey

There's something about the sorts of exclamations that have the satisfying abruptness of an actual swear word but aren't in fact rude – words like crikey!, blimey!, heck!, golly! and crumbs! – that appeals to the middle classes. Their antiquated charm makes them seem quaint and inoffensive, though many are actually blasphemy in disguise. According to the Collins dictionary, crikey = Christ; blimey = God blind me; heck = Hell; golly = God; crumbs = Christ, again.

These expressions are already particularly popular

with primary-school teachers who have more reason than most of us to swear, but who are bound by convention not to. Mind you, primary-school teachers probably derive more satisfaction from using the words as they're more likely than the rest of us to know what they mean. Maybe we should revive the notion of blasphemy to make the words themselves more edgy.

Totes amaze

What not to Say

'Totes amaze'

Takes you aback in its complete (or perhaps one should say 'totes') tastelessness. Sadly, we merely grin and bear it from others, perhaps for fear of being regarded as a fuddy-duddy.

'Boom'

The MCs can't get away with this sort of thing. It's unconvincing and, at worst, ridiculous. You might claim the defence of ironic usage, but that's just not true, is it?

'The thing is . . . is'

The thing is... is

The 'double is' is verbal clumsiness. Stop introducing comments and just say what the thing is.

'Haitch'

There's particular anxiety here because 'haitch' is accepted pronunciation in Irish speech. But you'll never find the letter H written as haitch, no matter how Irish your dictionary. 'Aitch' is the only acceptable MC pronunciation.

Haitch

Ha Ha Ha but Never LMFAO: How to be Middle-Class Online

The middle classes now have several ways of distinguishing our writing in emails, facebook updates, forums, tweets and text messages, though they are often as much a matter of what is *not* done as what is. This is our comprehensive MC guide to what to say online and how to say it.

General rules

Cutting vowels is OK, txtspk is not

When it comes to abbreviating words, there is a subtle,

unspoken rule that you will not use txtspk such as '2' for 'to', 'n' for 'and', or 'lol' for 'laughing out loud'. However, 'cd/wd' for 'could/would' is OK, as are acronyms *if* the expression is quite wordy: 'IMO' for 'in my opinion' passes, and you can just about get away with 'TBH' for 'to be honest' on a forum.

Mornings/afternoons

'This am/this pm' are OK: 'this aft' is not.

Upper case or lower case

'hi stuart, can you please fwd me the notes from that meeting, thanks, j' is happening more and more. It will either be interpreted as a sweet and quirky way of saying, 'We're on a level, this is just a gentle request, not an order', or as laziness; it might be assumed you're sending the message from a train and are too busy to bother putting in the capitals. Babyish or lazy; neither is particularly great. We recommend putting the uppers and lowers in the correct places.

The rules of email

First name once, then nothing

When beginning an email, 'Dear' is fuddy-duddy

unless an unusual occasion demands formality, but just going straight into the message is rude. The middle-class emailer has two choices, then: either to use the first name of the addressee on a line of its own, or to use 'Hi' and then the first name. The former is used by people hoping to appear forthright. Whatever the choice, you don't need a greeting at all once the exchange is under way.

Best, regs and KR

Proper valedictions are starting to be deemed too stuffy for business emails; not cool enough. 'Kind regs' or just 'regs' appear quite often, as does the particularly lifeless 'KR'. None of these actually conveys any kindness, or regards. Combine this with the new trend for putting an initial instead of your whole name, and the end of an email looks like some sort of code: 'KR, M'. 'Wishes' have been crushed out of use, too, and it's now just 'Best', which doesn't mean anything at all on its own. Best to avoid it altogether and put 'Thanks' and then your name.

The initial sign-off

The single initial has a secretive, intimate edge –

similar to saying, 'Hi, it's me' on the phone. But it should definitely be kept for sign-offs. Don't address someone just by their initial – it sounds mocking, somehow.

The 'x' factor

First she addresses you by your first name in an email. Then you speak on the phone and she says, 'Leave it with me, darlin''. So far, so sweet. And then, the final insult: she (for it is always a she, somehow) signs off her latest message with an x after her name.

It would be fine if you knew or had even met this person. But a recruitment consultant trying to find you a job, or an estate agent managing the sale of your house? You wouldn't kiss them hello in person, so why is it that the innocent x is becoming more and more a feature of exchanges with a certain type of person?

We would suggest that texting is to blame. Since we don't need to sign off with our name (as the recipient presumably has it stored in his or her phone), an x is a convenient way to end the message. Or it's the more grown-up version of the dreaded emoticon. Either way, there's really no place for an x in business emails.

The Art of Middle-Class Social Networking

The Facebook walls of friends and friends-of-friends will turn up many different types of status update and digital intercourse. For today's manner-minding middle-class social networker, certain habits and forms of discourse are best left alone, lest others find them irritating or even offensive. Here we reveal some of the least desirable, as well as the more curious.

1 Cyber-Kyleing

As in *The Jeremy Kyle Show*, cyber-Kyleing is the act of having a full-blown row on your wall, possibly involving several friends and family members. Subjects may include infidelity, money, disputed guilt for a misdemeanour, or, in one instance, where various family members would be spending Christmas ('I cant b in seven places at once lol!').

2 Frape

Unpleasant but nevertheless commonly used term

for posting on someone's wall under their identity, by sneaking onto the computer while they are logged in but out of the room. May be light and humorous ('I smell!'), or inflammatory ('I want the world to know I am a dirty cheat and seeing other women'). The latter type tends to lead to cyber-Kyleing.

3 Wonderwalling

This involves florid declarations of love, which broach the British antipathy towards the overuse of emotional language in public. Tends to read like randomly cut-up Hallmark Valentine's card greetings. 'U r the sun, the stars in the sky, my life my soul I luv u babe xx'. It is a rule of middle-class life that you don't do this sort of thing. The more verbose statements of love tend to be made by men, with female partners responding gratefully: 'Aw thanks hun luv u'. This basic pattern can form a lengthy replies list, with friends adding 'Get a room lol' at the bottom.

4 Avatarism

The creation of a profile for a fictional character. Frequently adopted by dog and cat owners, who pose as their pets talking about themselves. Can be charming. Or not.

5 Coelhoism

The posting of status updates consisting of deep philosophical statements of the kind associated with author Paulo Coelho, usually linked by an ellipsis to another statement about the poster's own life and feelings, e.g. 'Everything on earth is being continuously transformed because the earth is alive and has a soul. . . so true, we are all in a constant state of flux . . . but we can still love each other, to all my friends xxx'.

6 Conspicuous Self-Locating

Regularly announcing that you are in a fashionable place, possibly doing interesting things. 'Just been 2 gallery, now in Gdansk Bar in Shoreditch. Cool.' May get competitive if other Conspicuous Self-Locators get involved ('Gdansk Bar is sh** now').

7 The Zombie Call

Lengthy post on your wall from ancient acquaintance whose friend request you wish you had not accepted. Full of questions. He or she wants to know how you are and to ask if they can live next door to you in

Farmville. It looks bad if you reply to everyone else but him/her, and yet you don't want to encourage them. Tricky.

And here are three essentially harmless and quite comforting forms of Facebook conversation:

1 Concept Updates
The concept update is a single word or short phrase, apparently chosen at random. 'Bitterness'; 'Take me'; 'Unexpected item in bagging area', and so on. Favoured by the more creative user.

2 Trivving
Taking part in the long discussions of trivial, mundane detail (biscuits, TV, pop-music minutiae) to which Facebook seems so well suited.

3 Happy Mundanities
Regular announcements of new mundane activities undertaken. 'Just had coffee mmm'; 'Ready for wine, lol!'; 'Late for work' and so on. Should be dull and yet much of Facebook's success could be down to the fact that in reality they are strangely comforting to read.

Five Things not to do on Twitter

The art of being middle-class on Twitter really involves many more don'ts than dos. It is very easy to be a good, decent, middle-class tweeter if you make sure that, at all costs, you don't commit any of the five heinous crimes below against Twitter culture and etiquette.

1 Spout inspirational/philosophical/religious quotations

Twitter is absolutely riddled with tweets issued by people who have nothing of any note to say for themselves, and who instead spout sickly, nauseating quotations about love, life and the universe. This goes against every middle-class sensibility and it is unacceptable.

2 Retweet nice things said about you, including #ff

If someone tweets you on the public timeline to congratulate you on something, e.g. they liked your latest blog post, thought your new book was excellent, think you're just a brilliant person generally, *do not* retweet this to all of your followers. This might seem like obvious advice, but we're afraid to say it happens all the time, even to supposedly sensible people. It looks arrogant and desperate, and it is exactly the same as saying, 'Someone thinks I'm awesome, you should all take note'. If someone pays you the compliment of recommending you to their followers using the 'Follow Friday' custom, it is reprehensible to retweet this to all of your followers. Be cool.

3 Retweet celebrities

Dear oh dear, this is another one that seems so bloody obvious we can't quite believe we have to say it. Middle-class people should never, *ever* retweet something said by a celebrity. If people want to hear what celebrities have to say on Twitter, they are free to follow them, and actually most middle-class tweeters don't. Nobody needs you to retweet something Stephen Fry said. And if you think retweeting Stephen (along with millions of other people) will get his attention and encourage him to follow you, then you need to pull yourself together.

4 Conduct your actual, real social life via tweets

Nobody wants to hear where you're hanging out and who with. That's what public figures do on Twitter and that's why they are, largely, dull people to follow. As a clever, media-literate middle-classer, you should be using Twitter to comment wryly on the latest news and play politically relevant word games. 'I had an AMAZEBALLS day with @bezziemate on Kings

Road, see you again soon hun'. None of that, please. Save it for Facebook, or preferably save it completely.

5 Be more aggressive/honest than you would in your real life
Yes, Twitter gives you the capability to express every thought and opinion that comes into your head during the day, but you should definitely not exercise it. (Unless you're tweeting under a pseudonym or an assumed personality – in which case, do what you like and have fun.) You should still observe real-world middle-class social laws – don't, for example, tweet too much information to your one thousand followers about your ill health and chart every visit to the doctor. Don't take to Twitter after a bad break-up to tell the world how upset you are. *Do not* moan about your job and your boss. And don't be more aggressive/blunt/insulting than you would in real life. Basically, anything you wouldn't be prepared to say, using your actual voice, on the phone to someone you don't know, should not be said in a tweet.

Holding your Breath when you Check your Messages

The next time you sit down at your laptop to check

your email, or look at your BlackBerry, or even 1571
your landline, try to notice your breathing. Or rather
not-breathing — because the chances are that, when
you first clock that little screen and wonder what's
coming, you pull that momentary little freeze-face.
You know the one: eyes unblinking; shoulders slightly
tensed; mouth open a centimetre or so, feeling a
mixture of trepidation and fear. Will it all be shite
work emails, or will a friend have sent something
funny? Some project that's gone through quicker than
you thought, or something that's gone wrong? All
spam, or something glam?

Techno freeze-face seems an entirely new middle-
class phenomenon. True, we used to wait for the
postman on days when he was bringing important
news, but we didn't sit by the letterbox half a dozen
times a day. That would have been seen as unhealthy,
and quite rightly so. It isn't good for you to tense
up and stop breathing, either. But perhaps we
don't think about it because there are worse things
troubling us. The small panic attack and indecision
we experience when receiving a phone call with no
number displayed is far worse, for starters.

Chapter 4

How to Think

The middle-class mind works in overdrive, questioning, self-analysing, often beating itself up. There are very few actions the MCs will take without our minds entering into extensive pre- and post-analysis and there are some thought processes that are simply uniquely, brilliantly middle class. What are the essential MC virtuous miseries? Why does a trip round the supermarket cause such angst? Why do we feel the need to apologise for perfectly reasonable requests? In this chapter we're on the couch. And the first talking point addresses the middle-class aversion to book recommendations.

Love Book-Recommending, Hate Being the Recommendee

Book-recommending is an unstoppable behaviour among the middle classes. But the truth of the matter is that everyone likes recommending, but it's awkward and kind of tedious being the recommendee.

Book-recommending is one of the smuggest sensations readily available to a middle-class person. 'Oh, you just *have* to read this. I literally couldn't put it down; it's got the *most* richly drawn characters. I've already recommended it to Paul and Tabs, and even Mum's going to try it and she only reads crime.' Yes, the book recommendation comes with a great deal of gushing, and a huge amount of self-satisfaction.

Through all the gushing, what the recommendee hears is this: 'I feel amazing about the fact that I've finished this book, and I want to show off to you that I've read it so that you associate me with this book, the greatness of which is widely acknowledged.'

And as the recommendee, you say: 'Wow, it sounds absolutely amazing, that'll be next on my bedside table', and you have no intention of following it up. Because, of course, you're too busy thinking of another book to recommend competitively in turn.

The Twelve Virtuous Miseries

A virtuous misery can be defined as: something you slog through glumly in the belief that, as it is supposed to be classic, or it's been heavily hyped up, it must be in some way good for you and therefore you should try to appreciate it. We have compiled an absolutely unscientific list of twelve. You should consider this list a definitive guide to what you must attempt to read, watch, eat and listen to, no matter how painful the experience. But just know that we understand why they make you miserable.

12 Chekhov plays

Unbearably worthy. Withnail had it spot on: 'Always full of women staring out of windows, whining about ducks going to Moscow.'

11 Ulysses

You understand why it's important, you know the writing is amazing, yet you can't get past page 100 despite trying on and off since graduating from an English course twenty years ago.

10 Any type of exercise in the home

You've got various fitness DVDs – the latest one is a zumba. You've spent a fortune on all the gadgets and gimmicks like chest expanders and stomach flatteners. You know it's a good use of your time at home, but it feels totally ridiculous jumping about and stretching in your own living room. Not to mention impossible to continue past the eight-minute mark without the peer pressure of an instructor or onlookers to keep you motivated.

9 Inception

The bit where the city folded up was fantastic . . . otherwise, very silly indeed. None of it seemed particularly dreamlike, and the smart-arse exchanges between the dream-team buddies were extremely annoying. The snow-battle sequence was like watching someone playing that Halo video game. Bit boring, to be honest.

8 Any well-regarded, hyped-up historical book

You know you really should have read them. And you probably own pretty much all of them. The Stalin ones, that Stalingrad one, *London: The Biography*, the Samuel Pepys biog, the Byron one. You've tried your very best to plough through each one, but sorry, *you just can't*.

7   Fine dining

Yes, it's food at its best and most creative, but honestly, who apart from some stuck-up smug git would want to go to a Michelin-starred restaurant where the ambiance is like God's waiting room and be served, for silly money, self-indulgent food in kiddie-sized portions by some chef who would much rather be on telly anyway?

6   Bob Dylan

You do love his sixties and seventies work but it's all a bit too much, what with the literary and philosophical merits and the political messages and, frankly, it's too earnest and, ultimately, hard work.

5   SLR cameras

All that hocus-pocus about aperture and distance, interchangeable lenses and shutter lags. It's all arse. Give us our Panasonic Lumix back.

4 Westerns

Every proper film buff, director and
critic bangs on about cowboy films.
Once Upon a Time in the West, *Hud*, *The
Wild Bunch*, *The Unforgiven*. Has anyone
actually managed to sit through a whole
one until the end? The best cowboy is
clearly Woody from *Toy Story*.

3 Japan

Everyone seems to love Japan. Yes, Tokyo has
great shops and nice food. And few of us could go
untouched by the grace and stoicism the country
showed in the wake of the tsunami. However,
the architecture is underwhelming. The rules and
manners are ridiculously rigid, making the people
appear sad, uptight and somewhat repressed. The
atmosphere is fun-free. And oranges cost five quid
each. It's the anti-Italy.

2 The Pregnant Widow by Martin Amis

All that hype for a book that was really just what-
me-and-my-posh-friends-did-on-holiday *forty sodding
years ago*. Three hundred pages leading up to a big

Atonement-style turning point that was actually so understated it was barely noticeable.

1. Food Doctor

We thought it was just their 'healthy bagels – an exciting sandwich alternative!' that made our hearts sink, but actually it's everything about Food Doctor, with their sad, medical-looking packaging which is the colour of hospital gowns, and annoyingly chirpy brand voice that uses an excessive number of exclamation marks.

'Sorry To Bother You, But May I . . .?'

MCs are never more than a few minutes from our next apology. We apologise before, during and after the smallest of everyday things, particularly when asking for something. For example, you might have queued patiently for a while in a coffee shop, holding the panini you've chosen from the counter. When it's your turn, you find yourself physically cringing as you hand the panini to the barista, and you hear yourself saying, 'Can I be awkward and have this toasted?'

Hyper-awareness of creating any sort of inconvenience for, or demanding something from, someone – especially a person in a service role – is common among our kind. Demands and requests without any sort of embedded apology make a middle-class person very uncomfortable, often actually cross. Sorry we all feel so 'sorry' for asking for things – but we hope you don't lose this characteristic as it's actually quite lovely.

Inventing Things to Worry About When there's Nothing Wrong

Despite the fact that most of us seem to love smartphones, we also spend a lot of time complaining about how they cause more stress in our daily lives. People from work can always get hold of you; you can't help looking at your emails even though you know it will ruin your weekend; friends tell you about their latest apps rather than their news. And so on.

A study by Worcester University revealed that people were actually suffering from smartphone withdrawal, which raises the following points: a) we all secretly enjoy being stressed, and b) as a result we now invent things to be stressed about. We have identified these five emerging middle-class stresses that could soon rival that identified by the Worcester study.

1 *Fake sincerity anxiety:* crops up when everyone who came to your dinner party says they enjoyed it and the food was nice, so you worry that they're just being polite.

2 *Inverted laziness:* the nagging feeling that comes when your boss hasn't overloaded you with extra work this week, meaning you worry that they're not happy with the work you've done.

3 *Punctuality fear:* the stress resulting from the Ocado delivery actually arriving on time when you had banked on it being late.

4 *Deceptive discipline syndrome:* occurs when your children have been really well behaved, so you worry that they're hiding the fact that they've done something wrong.

5 *Tradesman suspicion:* results from workmen finishing the job in your house on time and on budget, so you fret that they haven't done the job properly.

Ordinary, Working-Class Pleasures that are Enjoyed by the Middle Classes in a Special Way

The middle classes love nothing more than taking something apparently working-class, naff and trashy and extracting some sort of surprisingly enjoyable, intellectually informed, possibly ironic frisson from it. There are a few different forms of this:

- *A poshed-up rebranding of a formerly downmarket thing:* 'Did you know that the spa at Center Parcs has won a *Vogue* magazine award?'
- *A Nigel Slater-ish championing of a cheap and cheerful, boldly non-organic foodstuff:*

  'I just can't get enough Heinz tomato soup/ tinned chocolate puddings/ Tunnock's Teacakes/ builder's tea.'
- *A thing for kitschy bargains:*

  'Ooh, we love a pound shop, don't we, Sophie?'

The working classes are at liberty to watch, eat and enjoy things unhindered by prejudice, over-consideration, satire and significance. With the MCs, it's complicated and self-congratulatory. Often, cod expertise and a trained eye are hinted at, as follows:

- *Jordan:* 'You know, if you take away the tranny make-up and ridiculous tits, Katie is actually a very beautiful girl.'

- *The X Factor:* 'You've got to hand it to Cowell; it's a brilliant business he has there.'

A deeper commitment, with a self-consciously Alan Bennett-esque twist, is the irony-tinged weekend spent at a traditional British seaside resort. The working classes go to Margate or Brighton or Scarborough in the summer because they have fun at the slot machines and enjoy the fish and chips, but the middle-class visit – in the harsher winter months, mostly – is more high-minded, soundtracked by that 'sand dunes and salty air' ditty by Groove Armada. They love the fact that Tracey Emin has a place in Margate and that Fat Boy Slim and Julie Burchill both live in Brighton ('Brighton has always had a great literary scene').

These are the essential elements of the irony-tinged seaside weekend:

- Seeking out *the best* fish and chips ('Not actually Rick Stein's restaurant, but this simple shack we found on the beachfront' – actually it was recommended by *Guardian Weekend*).
- Taking tea and cakes and bracing walks on the pier, all the while enjoying the wonderful *cheapness* of

the amusement arcades and thrill rides.

- Frequent attempts at taking Martin Parr-type photos.

The Middle-Class Index Card Fetish

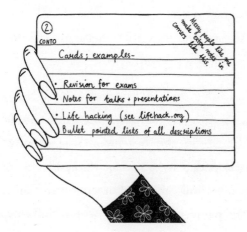

① The middle-class index-card fetish

Have you noticed that, while stationery in general is quite a big middle-class obsession, index-cards in particular have remained popular long after their original function was usurped by computer software?

Middle class people love using index- PTO ➜

② CONTO

Many people like me make corner notes in corners like this.

Cards; examples-

- Revision for exams
- Notes for talks + presentations
- Life hacking (see lifehack.org)
- Bullet pointed lists of all descriptions

Why We Can't Stop Talking About China

At middle-class dinner parties, it's becoming common for the conversation to be taken over abruptly and completely by China and its booming luxury goods market. Then you get stuck on it for what seems like three days, caught in an endless barrage of half-remembered statistics from the *Economist* and people saying, 'Yes, Tom worked in Beijing for three months, he said it was amazing, sixty people crowded into one single bed in a railway siding,' and so forth. This sort of China-drone, with people harping on about how 'everything's going East', is becoming the new house-prices conversation for middle-class get-togethers – and it somehow manages to be even more boring. You should consider a move to Shanghai just to get away from it.

The Curious Attraction of Other People's Shower Gel

Popping to the loo or having a shower when you're staying at someone else's house is, for the MCs, an opportunity to check out all the bathroom products they have – and, ultimately, to make judgements about the people based on what you find. You know

this because you're very anxious about your own products when people spend time in the bathroom at your house. You want to provide the best handwash, ideally from quite an obscure source, with a rare fragrance. You always double-check what products you have on show on the shelf, around the bath and on the shower rack – and of course swivel the best ones round so that their labels are on display.

On exiting the bathroom, it's very MC to comment on the lovely handwash, shower gel or whatever it is you've used. In fact, you should always make a point of doing so. Try something like: 'Your handwash is absolutely gorgeous. What an unusual fragrance – it somehow reminds me of last summer in Kefalonia.' If you're the host and your guest doesn't comment on your products when they come out of the bathroom, it's understandable that you'll feel bereft, cheated and unfulfilled. It's definitely OK to prompt them: 'Did you have a try of that lovely shower gel I left by the bath for you? Unusual fragrance, isn't it . . .?'

Supermarket Angst

For some people, supermarkets are a consumer paradise, but for others they are purgatory. Along with the many other unpleasant emotions they can inspire: extreme disorientation, paralysing confusion when contemplating the biscuits/cheese/detergent options, and plain old rage, the biggest is anxiety. Anxiety about making sure all your purchases are bagged up before the cashier hands you your change and receipt. His or her outstretched palm hanging silently and ponderously in the air as you frantically struggle to squeeze, say, some leeks into the space between a cereal box and some tins of tomato, while the people in the queue behind regard you with a

combination of impatience, loathing and naked pity. 'Oh for f***'s sake,' you can almost hear them thinking, 'get on with it, you imbecile.'

It may be an imagined anxiety – a bit like those dreams where you realise you're in a pub or at work without any trousers on – but the feeling seems real enough: of being scrutinised, judged and found wanting as a competitor in the consumer-human race. People hate queueing in supermarkets; we have all at some point regarded the fumbling, stressed shopper ahead with something approaching hatred for not being fast enough to get their shopping bagged up, paid for and out of there.

It is not, of course, the cashier's fault. They're only doing their job, efficiently relieving shoppers of their cash and processing them through the system. Nor is it the fault of the people queueing, even if they don't smile much while you are struggling with the shopping. (There is of course a second stage to this – the fear of keeping people waiting while you stuff your change and receipts into the correct compartment of your wallet or purse before finally leaving. This can occasionally take a few terror- and shame-filled moments to complete.) Still, it's one of those very modern, anxiety-creating experiences that add an extra piquancy to the misery of late-consumerist life.

To help the moment pass as smoothly as possible for all concerned, follow our foolproof three-point plan:

1 Get yourself prepared while you're in the queue. Load your shopping onto the conveyor in the exact order you want to bag it up. Sort your purse/wallet out so that it's ready for when you need to get cash and stuff receipts in.

2 Smile at the person in the same situation in front of you, in the hope that the person behind you will sympathise in a similar way.

3 On no account take ages at the post-bagging stage, e.g. placing coins in the zipped compartment of your purse, straightening notes and receipts before sliding them neatly into your wallet, fiddling with your bag to find a suitable corner for your purse. If you do this, you're in the way, aren't you? The person behind you will be getting very anxious as their shopping begins piling up in the bagging area before they can get there and that's not on.

CHAPTER 5

Domestic Dilemmas: How to Make Yourself at Home

The middle classes aren't even truly relaxed in their own homes, you know. The domestic sphere is riddled with dilemmas and issues. The unbearable untidiness of the airing cupboard and the urge to tidy it up before the cleaner arrives; the relationship battleground that is the dishwasher; the cooker hood as a powerful kitchen status symbol. These issues are ever present in middle-class home life, and it can only get worse when you invite someone into your home. Let's start by having a look at a central middle-class question.

Why do Middle-Class People Hide their Pants?

The idea of hanging pants out on the line makes middle-class people uncomfortable. You might have noticed that the people who live in the council estate down one side of your street happily hang their underthings out to dry, while those in the large private houses on the other side don't even put them in their back gardens. Perhaps it's a subtle way of demonstrating that one owns a tumble dryer. If you're going to be brave and drape your pants over a clothes horse in your garden, we suggest you make sure they are mostly Marks & Spencer smalls.

The Cooker Hood: A Rising Star Among Middle-Class Kitchen Status Symbols

Cooker hoods are becoming more and more adventurous and powerful as an expression of middle-classness. We have cottoned on to the fact that a classy hood definitely adds value to a house, but some might say it's getting a bit out of hand. These days we don't just have the steel and curved-glass chimney-effect hoods, but also elaborate cylindrical affairs above island hobs, hoods in different colours

– mainly red – hoods disguised by fake Victorian mantelpieces around the cooker and various curvy, brushed-steel models. They have become more outlandish as time has passed. If you're looking for a really solid kitchen status symbol, the creative cooker hood is where it's at.

You find yourself in the market for a cooker hood, but which of the daunting range of models will you go for? You could take the sensible, scientific route of buying a copy of *Which?* and researching matters such as decibels, extraction power, warranties, reliability, customer feedback and so on, or you could ask what you want your hood to say about you and take it from there. Follow our handy guide:

Chimney cooker hoods

The most quintessentially MC of cooker-hood variants, offering the widest choice and the necessary girth to deal with your five- or six-ring range.

Subgenre 1: the pitched-roof stainless-steel chimney hood
It might not be a Smeg, but even if it isn't, you hope people think it is. Not because you've done your research and found the brand to be better than others;

it's just important to be seen as the sort of person who would choose a Smeg (or Neff or Bosch) cooker hood over, say, a Hotpoint. You desperately want your kitchen to look like the sort of place in which Giorgio Locatelli might get busy on some osso buco, but you also know that it's not necessary to actually cook in order to enjoy a shiny stainless-steel cooker hood.

MC points: *****

Subgenre 2: the curved-glass chimney hood

By going with a semi-invisible material and the softer lines of the curve, you are clearly slightly uncomfortable with showiness and bold design statements. You might be more *Livingetc* than *Wallpaper**, but we salute your MC reserve.

MC points: ***

Subgenre 3: own-brand

Lazy, lazy, lazy. If you've gone with the off-the-peg hood on offer with your IKEA fitted kitchen, you are just not trying. We can only assume you're doing up the kitchen simply to try to sell the house.

MC points: **

Island cooker hoods

The big boys of the cooker-hood world. The largest and most powerful. The mere fact that you have a kitchen big enough to accommodate a cooking 'island', or that you are even going to call it an 'island' at all, speaks volumes about your priorities and your lifestyle. It's a hood that makes a statement, but it was probably chosen for you by the architect you got to knock through to your side return, install a strip of roof lights and fit sliding glass doors opening onto the garden.

MC points: *****

Off-piste cooker hoods

Why have a cooker hood that looks like a cooker hood when it could look like a crystal light fitting or a wall-mounted modernist sculpture? Aspirational Italian brand Elica can supply you with either, and more. For a mere £1.5K. Or you can subvert the standard shapes by going for them in white (for diehard minimalists), black (gay men and people who want something to match the Aga) or statement colours (subscribers to *World of Interiors*). Your kitchen looks stunning; shame you spend more time in restaurants.

MC points: ***

Built-in

You've bypassed the modern industrial aesthetic and gone for something more country kitchen. Maybe your units are called something like Shaker or Windsor. You probably learned to cook with your mum and now produce wholesome food every day, not just to impress your friends. You uphold a reverence for Delia. We imagine you bake really nice cakes.

MC points: ***

Visor/free-standing

Generally the cheapest and least powerful option. No chimney. No shiny acreage. Just a thin panel sticking out from the wall above a sad four-ring hob. Reeks of rented accommodation. On the plus side, you are probably young and unencumbered enough to go out for the evening instead of worrying about what to cook for supper.

MC points: **

But don't worry about how many stars you got. The mere fact that you even care about things like cooker hoods is enough to make you a card-carrying member of the middle classes.

The Overhead Light: Emergency Use Only

When you wander down the street in the evening, it's alarming how many front rooms are lit up like office corridors. How unwelcoming and uncomfortable it looks in there. Such harsh lighting ruins the mood, shows up too much detail. The overhead light – the 'big light' – is one of those great dividers of people.

It bewilders a middle-class person that some

people use the 'big light' in their homes, and it's particularly horrifying in the dining room. The 'big light' should only be used as a sort of emergency light source, when there's a broken glass or something that needs clearing up. It's not at all appropriate for everyday – or every night – lighting. It's candles and low lamps all the way for middle-class homes.

The Fine Art of Concealing a Sky Dish

Sky TV seems to be becoming acceptable for the middle classes, but there is one very strict condition: the dish has to be hidden from view, i.e. not stuck on the side of the house. After a little non-scientific research, we have discovered the top five locations for concealment:

1 *Flat roof:* ideal, though a bit embarrassing if the man who comes to fix it says he just puts his on the wall.

2 *Garden shed:* quite appealing, as it could make the neighbours think you have Sky in the shed, which is impressive. Wiring is an issue, though.

3 *Back of house:* fine if you have no houses behind, obviously. But reveals how conscious you are of other people's opinions.

4 *Garden wall:* we are sceptical, but we have seen one on a wooden frame in a garden.

5 *Neighbour's house:* i.e. paying a neighbour to suffer the indignity on your behalf. Never actually been tried, as far as we know. And not really worth it, as one doesn't want to live *next* to a dish either.

Central-Heating Anxiety

Central-heating anxiety rears its ugly head in middle-class homes in November, persists through the winter, almost ruins Christmas Day ('We really don't need the heating on, Martin, the oven's been on for two hours; I'm cooking as thoroughly as the goose'), and only finally subsides in March.

We are uncomfortable with central heating. We

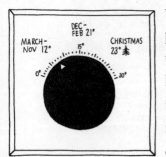

want warm homes but feel an intense pressure not to get at the thermostats unless absolutely necessary. For our kind, there is a perceived nobility in waiting as long as possible and we'll revel in telling our friends the exact date we finally gave in. Enjoy this feeling and radiate smugness as you talk of preferring to 'snuggle up' in a blanket and 'curl up with a cup of cocoa', all the while knowing you were freezing your middle-class bottom off.

How to Impress the Babysitter

Middle-class mums have a very awkward relationship with babysitters. The impulse is to attempt to show off Mary Poppins-esque parenting skills. Why do working mums feel the need to present this flaky snapshot – wittering on about organic Ribena and our 'aversion' to TV? Because we are constantly proving ourselves, that's why – and not only to other mums. There's little point in our telling you not to try to impress your babysitter – we know it's an irresistible urge. Instead, here are some strategies you might not have thought of:

- Have a range of activities ready and set up for the babysitter to lead, such as a table crammed with potato stamps, paint and glitter.
- Accompany the visual effect with comments like: 'It's important for kids still to make things these days, don't you think?'

- Hide any modern stuff that might associate you with lazy parenting, e.g. kick the Nintendo DS and DVDs under the sofa before the babysitter arrives.

Three Ways to Meet the Neighbours

We've all seen those American films in which newcomers to a neighbourhood are greeted with fresh-baked pies and cheery introductions from the folks next door, but very few home-movers have experienced this in Britain. The British middle classes are more diffident; not so much antisocial as socially anxious, worried that the new people might be busy, or not keen on meeting at the moment. This easily lapses into not-really-knowing-the-neighbours, which we don't want either. Is there a way, perhaps, to manage the situation from the newcomers' side? Anything you can do to make friends as you move in? Well, yes, actually. We have three tips:

1 Appeal for help
The British might be shy, but they are great in crises – not least because crises are an excuse to overcome shyness. So asking for help might well get the ball

rolling, and will be a lot less awkward than saying, 'Hi, we've just come to introduce ourselves . . .' When you move in, go round and ask for as much help as you dare; the name of a good plumber is the most basic and will lead to conversations about local services. Tools are the next step up (but you *must* return them), and if they are parents of strapping lads and lasses, physical help getting furniture upstairs is always an icebreaker – and gives an opening for a small, follow-up gift (wine is fine – and have a glass if they offer to open it when you're there).

2 Be gauche

Unless they were on close terms with the former residents, your neighbours will be curious about the inside of your house – *everyone* is curious about the inside of other people's houses, hence the huge number of magazines featuring them.

3 Wait until Christmas

If you're confident and chatty, you can invite the neighbours to a little drinks party and Bob's your uncle. If you're not, such events can be slightly excruciating. Our advice is to wait until December and do one then. Christmas throws up endless topics of conversation (families, travel, mulled-wine recipes) and, as it's a busy time, no one will mind if you wrap things up early – useful if neighbours turn out to be less-than-ideal company.

The Unbearable Untidiness of Airing Cupboards

Getting fresh bedding from the airing cupboard is one of life's small yet potent irritations. The sheet, quilt and pillowcase sets are never grouped together, and extracting them makes everything begin to fall out so that you have to jam it all back in in a right mess. About once a month you take it all out and stack it in afresh, but it always ends up like this, doesn't it? And you can't help feeling that it's a deep personal failing.

We're all convinced we remember our mum's airing cupboard as a little cave of domestic tranquillity. The contrast between hers and yours is a marker of the divide between the simpler, poorer but happier world of our childhoods, and the better-off-but-never-feeling-properly-on-top-of-things one we inhabit now.

And isn't it always a total mess when the cleaner comes, making you worry she'll judge you, therefore causing you to argue with your other half about whether it wouldn't just be less stressful not to have a cleaner at all?

Tricky relationship, you and your cleaner. You shouldn't feel guilty about having one, though; you work hard. But for some reason, interacting with her is fraught with tensions, mainly because you have a whole load of things you'd like to ask her to do or change but you don't want to seem fussy. Here are ten issues you wish you could ask your cleaner not to do:

1   Skipping cleaning the cooker hood.
2   Polishing the wooden floors so they're dangerously slippery.
3   Arranging the cushions on the sofas too symmetrically.
4   Putting coffee-table books back on the bookshelves.
5   Vacuuming right between the banister spindles.
6   Vacuuming under the cast-iron radiators.
7   Bringing her own non-green cleaning products and ignoring your Ecover and Method bottles.

8 Putting the Le Creuset casserole pot away when it belongs on the range.
9 Parking her car half on the pavement when there's plenty of room on the road.
10 Not charging a round number so we never have the right money

The best way to handle this is to make sure you're out when the cleaner comes. That way, you can leave a note outlining any or all of the above issues and come back to a tidy house without having had to confront her. You can't avoid her for ever, though; whether you like it or not, there is a point in the year when you'll need to pull yourself together. Don't worry, we're on hand to help.

What to Give the Cleaner for Christmas

Choosing a Christmas gift for someone who does regular work for you doesn't have to be the nightmare it may appear to be. The key thing is to be aware of the message you send with the present – which is something much bigger than 'Merry Christmas'.

For cleaners – this really is a simple principle –

choose gifts that show an awareness of the life they lead beyond cleaning your house. It's not witty or endearing to give them novelty Marigolds, take our word for it. Choose something luxurious, pampering or edible.

Gardeners might be more amenable to gifts that are a 'comment' on the service they provide for you: Gardener's Hand Cream could be a winner – and very useful, actually.

Definitely don't buy your piano tuner stationery/ an umbrella/tote bag with musical motifs on it; musicians hate this stuff. As with the cleaner, go for luxurious and/or edible. The definitive classless Christmas gift is a scented candle. Can't go wrong. Unless you employ a candlestick-maker.

The Dishwasher: a Relationship Battleground

Filling the dishwasher is more than a division of labour for most couples; it's a relationship battleground. It seems that in every couple one partner reckons they are better at loading the dishwasher than the other, or anyone else for that matter – the Dishwasher

Geek. The level of anxiety of the Dishwasher Geek is inversely proportional to the amount of space left in the machine. Like trying to squeeze onto an overcrowded commuter train, surely it's better to wait for the next load than to waste time playing some sort of crockery jigsaw puzzle?

The truly expert DG can part-load the dishwasher in such a way as to be able to anticipate the spatial requirements of further items. This ability seems to be absent in lesser mortals and it is this that leads to the frustration of having to rearrange dishes.

There's also a quandary of how to place items in the cutlery basket (for those households not fortunate enough to own a Miele with a cutlery tray). We recommend a tines- and points-down policy. Some say this inhibits cleaning, but we think all in all it's better to have to wash an item again than run the gauntlet of sharps every time the basket requires emptying. Needless to say, items should be placed with their kin to enable simple egress and a return to the cutlery drawer without having to sort them first.

Spotting a Dishwasher Geek in any couple is easy – after dinner at their house, offer to load their machine for them. At first they will politely decline assistance, and when you ignore them and start loading plates the wrong way round they will begin the first stages of a panic attack, as their steel and ceramic universe falls apart. It's a good idea to stop loading at this point, if you ever want to be invited to dinner again.

How to Hang an England Flag on your House

Don't be silly.

CHAPTER 6

How to be Middle Class at Work

How do you navigate all the tensions of the modern workplace with middle-class aplomb? The minutiae of getting through the work day can be overwhelming: the biscuit plate that stays entirely undisturbed for a three-hour management meeting; the difficult micro-moment at a business lunch when you're asked a question just as you've taken a bite of food; the impulse to show off your expensive pen whenever possible. Why have we become so competitive in the way we greet each other? And what phrases should you say in order to get the maximum middle-class martyr points for coming to work when you're ill? Read on for our complete guide to being middle class at work.

Being Asked a Question While you're Eating

In a business lunch scenario, it's very awkward to be asked a question at precisely the point that you've inserted a large forkful of food into your mouth. This moment ranks highly in the middle-class awkwardness index because there is no standard procedure. But there are five potential ways you could handle it:

1 Point to your chewing mouth and perform a small shrug as if to invite understanding on the basis of shared humanity. 'Hey,' this seems to say, 'wouldn't you know it? It's that old question-just-as-I-put-the-food-in moment! One sec while I get rid of this, OK?' Not classy.

2 Chew strongly and decisively two or three times, swallow hard, then talk. This can make you seem assertive but there is a risk of not swallowing effectively and coughing, perhaps even showering your fellow diners with food. Awkward.

3 Nod ponderously as if weighing up the question before answering, while you are in fact thinking only of getting the food down as quickly as you can. This is a good alternative, but only works for serious questions; ruminating on the weather while you were on holiday is ridiculous.

4 Be rescued by the other person, who may be kind enough to notice what has happened and help out by expanding on their question until they see you have swallowed the food.

5 As with many such awkward occasions, the best option, if you can pull it off, is to strike an upper-middle attitude of slightly arrogant confidence and merely chew at your leisure as you would in any situation. It has a worldly maturity about it and implies that both you and your dining partner are

so at ease with eating in restaurants that you no longer even notice such inelegant moments.

How to Pull a 'Well-ie'

Now that the middle classes are increasingly paranoid about holding on to our jobs, we drag ourselves to work even at the height of a fever and pretend to be absolutely fine. We all used to be such excellent slackers. Taking a sickie was pretty much part of the monthly plan, a sneaky way to boost a meagre holiday allowance, an easy weekend extender. We

all used to be superb at acting ill on the phone and in person on the day we returned to work, to make it believable. Cough, cough . . . cough. These days, we're marvellous at taking a 'well-ie', crafty in our attempts to seem well even though we're practically delirious with germs. We struggle in, sneeze all over our keyboards, our red noses glowing under the office strip lighting – making everyone else ill while we're at it. Here are some key phrases to maximise your martyr status when pulling a 'well-ie':

- 'Got to soldier on'
- 'It's only a bit of a cold'
- 'There's just no time to be ill these days, is there?'
- 'Oh well, at least I'm making myself useful'
- 'I'd feel a lot worse if I was at home letting the team down'

The Art of Middle-Class Greeting

Nowadays, it's not enough to greet someone at work with a simple 'How are you?' and reply with 'All right, thanks' or 'Not bad'. To fit into the modern middle-class office, you'll need to say something a lot more effusive by way of greeting. It is as if the old sort of subtle competition over personal wealth and success at work has passed into welfare and happiness. Try these:

- '*Great* to see you! How's it going?'
- '*Really good*, thanks!'
- 'Things are great, *super-busy*, as ever!'

And make sure you know the rules about . . .

When to Kiss and when to Shake Hands

In the world of work, there is a growing number of vexatious kiss/shake hands points when one isn't quite sure what to do. What if you're meeting two people and you know one well, but have only just met the other – kiss the first and shake the second? For women, what if the bloke is a horrible lech? If you have several staff and are on kissing terms with the one who has been there the longest, what do you do at Christmas parties with the new arrivals?

Our unscientific research across European and UK business exposed three rather interesting points on the matter:

- Female professionals tend to kiss visiting foreign employees, but never the local ones.

- It seems to be acceptable to kiss familiar clients, but never colleagues.
- There is more kissing in the private sector than in the public sector.

And with that, we've probably made this even more confusing for you than it was before. What we suggest you do is impose a handshake-only regime in the near future. But be careful to watch out for . . .

The Short Handshake

You might find that you go to shake a man's hand only to find, for a half-second, that you haven't made contact with anything. This is because his hand was hardly extended at all, his elbow being pressed to his hip – in other words, he was doing the short handshake, a move encouraged in business psychology books teaching you how to get an advantage over people. The idea is that by forcing the other person to reach out, you are making them come into your space and getting them out of their comfort zone. This is supposed to put you in a position of power. Have your wits about you because more and more people are doing it lately as things get more competitive. And on no account start doing it yourself; you don't want to come across like an insecure tosser who spends their spare time reading business psychology books.

The Untouched Biscuit Plate

The lavishness of the biscuits and snacks offered in meetings in the last few years has increased at the same rate as the likelihood of anyone taking one has decreased. Tea and coffee are poured, small talk is shared and A5 pads with the company's logo are distributed. And still no one takes a biscuit. You might be tempted to be the first to break ranks, but it means asking someone to pass you the plate and that's just too awkward; you don't want to look greedy and the plate remains untroubled all through the stupid meeting.

A way around this is to smuggle in your own stash of custard creams and try to eat them secretly behind the A5 pads. It's not as if anyone ever does anything useful in most meetings anyway.

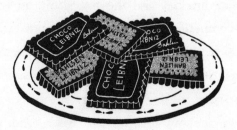

The Pen Moment

In business, The Pen Moment is when the need for a pen suddenly arises and everyone jumps to put forward their best pen as a sort of status symbol. Mont Blancs are the obvious status pen, and you might well have one yourself, but it is frustrating to have to wear them hidden on the inside of your jacket: three hundred quid and nobody can even see it! To get round this, produce said pen with a flourish at any opportunity – or, in meetings, ostentatiously place it on the table regardless of whether you're taking notes or not.

When Middle-Class People Wish they were Working Class: Envying the Blokes Waiting in the Van at 7.45 a.m.

Leaving for work at about a quarter to eight, you often see brickies and the like sitting in their van, waiting for eight o'clock so they can go in and start work – and this makes a middle-class person rather envious. Somehow they always look more relaxed, sitting there reading the paper and drinking coffee, than we feel on our way to work, and we envy

them that quiet roadside moment. As middle-class office workers, we don't get this sort of moment; if we did, we'd probably feel compelled to fill it by catching up on emails on our BlackBerry. Of course, the bloke in the van could just be bored, or wishing he'd left home ten minutes later, but still; from where we're standing (or walking past), that kerbside pause seems extremely desirable.

The Backlog of Crap, and the Luxury of Working on Trains and Planes

Many of us take out laptops or papers as soon as we board a train or plane, and then get down to serious work with a really engrossed and quite calm, happy expression on our faces. When you're on the train, you sort of have permission not to answer your phone or check email. Even if the train has wi-fi, there's still a consensus that while you're travelling, you're not available in the same way as usual. That means you can work, undisturbed, for a couple of hours. And that means you can tackle what all of us have these days: The Backlog of Crap.

The Backlog of Crap is the pile of emails, text

messages, facebook messages, reports that need checking and so on; it never quite goes away, but you always feel that with half a day's solid work you could clear it. Of course, we never get half a day to work solidly, because of interruptions, but a train (or even better, plane) journey makes us feel there is a chance.

The Extravagant Leaving Do

Although the more refined among us still sneer at the phenomenon, the extravagant celebration of milestone events has become a key part of mainstream middle-class life over the last decade. Significant birthdays, anniversaries, housewarmings and welcomes-home now seem quiet, bare affairs unless they involve elaborate surprises, shop-bought balloons and streamers, one-off cake toppers, specially printed t-shirts and gift collages compiled by the guests. Predictably, as every conventional milestone has been identified and commercialised, so new ones are being found and subjected to the same treatment; and most conspicuous among these is the extravagant work leaving do. It is part of a contemporary need to create a heightened, excited sense of reality closer to that of television. Here's how it's done:

- Key components: a card (signed by everyone, of course), multiple gateaux, much Prosecco into which everyone weeps, and a compilation CD of songs that meant something or other to people in the departee's department.
- Afterwards, everyone will go to the pub, drink hard for five hours and, in most cases, get off with other members of staff.
- The preparation takes about two weeks, and the discussion about the actual event lasts a good three days.

The proper thing to do as a middle-class person is to play along and enjoy it, while insisting that it's *soooo* sad and you will miss him/her *soooo* much and saying things like, 'Do you remember that time Rachel broke the photocopier with her lipstick?'

If you find yourself in the awkward position of being the departee, make sure you're sufficiently prepared for your leaving do. Your approach should include the following elements:

- A convincing 'I'm totally surprised, had no idea and I'm so incredibly touched' expression.
- 'A few words' of thanks and farewell prepared but designed to appear off-the-cuff.
- A vague sense that you're on the verge of tears. No need to actually cry, though. Bit much.
- Lots of writing down of personal email addresses because you're *absolutely sure* you'll stay in touch.

Offering to Get the Bill for Dinner When You Know Very Well that the Other Person is Going to Pay

At some point in a middle-class working life, there is a good chance that you will end up in a restaurant, eating a meal that you know the other person is going to pay for, and that, due to middle-class manners, you will make a show of being willing to pay. The general form is that your wealthier colleague or client will ask for the bill, and then, when it comes, ignore it until the conversation falls into a lull. Then he or she will take the small dish containing the bill and reach for their wallet. At this point, you should either offer verbally – 'Shall we split this?' – or (more middle class, since it relies on gesture, not speech), say nothing, but reach for your wallet with just a slight ostentation and slowness. The payer will notice this and, all being well, intervene with, 'Let me get this', or similar.

At this point, when the little awkwardness is dispelled, a verbal acknowledgement is required, with a tone of faux-delighted surprise: 'Are you sure?' (Oh, to hear someone say, 'Actually, now you mention it, no I'm not – let's go halves'!) There then follows a brief moment of relaxed bonhomie that may be possible only among the middle classes, as it is based on relief from certain social discomfort. 'Yes, yes, of course!' 'Oh, thank you very much!' 'You're very welcome!' and so forth.

This is what the fashionable philosopher Slavoj Žižek calls the offer-meant-to-be-refused; into the same category one might put offers of lending someone one's car, lending money or babysitting. They are more a part of middle-class existence than offering more tea to a visiting vicar.

Chapter 7

How to be Middle Class in Public

It's such hard work being a member of the public. There are so many obstacles: pedestrian crossings, noise, queues, other people. Other people! They're the worst. Why do people talk during films at the cinema and is there a polite way to get them to shut up? What do you do about the awkward bag on the seat, on the train? Is there an appropriate way to react when the person serving you in a shop answers their mobile phone while bagging up your items? Public life – simply being out and about – is a vulnerable, stressful place for the MCs. Let's all take a deep breath and find out how to navigate the big bad world.

The Awkward Bag-on-Seat Problem

The middle-class traveller is amazed by how often people place their bags on seats to try to ensure a double seat for themselves when the journey begins.

It's very English and uptight of us, but we never quite know what to say in this situation. You could go for a nice, indirect, 'Is anyone sitting there?' or go directly to, 'Can you move that bag, please?' On trying the former, you might find that you are lied to: the person says yes, as though someone else owned the bag, but then treats it as their own as the journey progresses. When trying the latter, you might find that you are just boldly ignored, which is very unsettling.

We propose the following method: a warm smile, followed with, 'Hi, could you move your bag so I can sit down, please?' The smiling greeting warms them up. 'Move your bag' is definite but subtle, and a smart 'please' rounds it off politely, making it hard to refuse.

How and When to Greet an Acquaintance When They're a Long Way Off

When you're walking down a long, straight street and you see an acquaintance – not a good pal, someone you know only vaguely – who is walking towards you but a long way off, what do you do? The way we see it, there are three possible ways to handle this:

- *Very awkward:* pretend not to have seen them at all. This is not what we advise – it makes it more uncomfortable for the other person, who in their own awkwardness might end up actually tapping you on the shoulder or calling your name as you walk by. It will inevitably mean having to engage in a lot of small talk and shuffling around on the pavement.

- *Quite awkward:* give a quick acknowledgement – a raised brow, perhaps – and then fix them in your view as you prepare to converge. You could go for this one, but it is quite intense and you'll probably find you start attempting to say 'hello', waving and making small talk a bit too soon, which makes other people on the street uncomfortable.

- *Least awkward, on balance:* smile and wave, and then avoid eye contact in the drawn-out minutes as you approach each other. Be nice, cheery and definite in the way you make the initial acknowledgement of recognition, then be cool, look away, look at your phone and then look up just a few seconds before you approach the person. This is perfect. Well, as perfect as an awkward middle-class moment can be.

Being Offended by a Simple Request for Directions

It might be a cliché to point out that MC people prefer to wander or drive around lost for hours on end rather than ask for directions, but it's true. We all recognise that vulnerability and gentle bruising of the ego that arises from having to give in and ask a stranger where something is. However, we MCs experience the same sense of shortcoming when the shoe's on the other foot and it's us being asked for directions.

We wonder why this stranger feels confident that we will know where Iceland is – do we look like we've shopped there? What does that say about us? Are we presenting ourselves wrongly? We'll feel disproportionately flattered to be asked for directions to somewhere cool, stylish or historical, but totally insulted to be asked where Halfords is. It's worth knowing this about yourself as a member of the neurotic middle classes, so that you can check your response next time you're asked directions to somewhere naff (don't panic, it really *isn't* a reflection on you, you know) or to somewhere cool (er, no, it's not because this stranger thinks you're the compass of cool, you're just the closest person on the street).

This list shows the places MC people like to be asked directions to, and those we categorically object to.

DON'T MIND BEING ASKED	HATE BEING ASKED
John Lewis	TK Maxx
Waitrose	Lidl
Quirkily-named gastropub	Wetherspoons
Art gallery	Amusement arcade
Southwold	Southend
Pizza Express	Pizza Hut
Whistles	JD Sports
Oddbins	Subway
Farmers' market	Iceland
Any delicatessen	Greggs
Marks & Spencer	Argos
Malmaison	Travelodge

Don't Hold your phone Funny

We had thought that it was only contestants on *The Apprentice* and kids on the bus who held their mobiles horizontally in front of their mouths in order to talk into them, but we're increasingly spotting this happening in 'real life'. Stop it. It looks ridiculous.

How to Play 'Coffee Chicken' in Train Stations

The young boy's game of chicken – i.e. standing in front of an oncoming vehicle for as long as you dare before leaping from its path – is of course not a popular one with modern middle-class adults, but we do have our own version. 'Coffee Chicken' is played in pairs on the concourses of railway stations. Here's how the game unfolds:

- To begin, two people who are catching a train together that leaves in approximately five to ten minutes both queue to buy a coffee.
- If the queue moves slowly, one of the pair will eventually give in and say, 'Let's leave it and get on,' whereupon the other will insist that they have plenty of time, even if the barista is going slowly.
- The tension escalates until either the worrier wins by persuading the coffee-wanter that they really have to go, or the coffee-wanter triumphs by sticking it out and landing their skinny cap – whereupon they . . .
- Both have to run to get the train that is by this stage about to pull out.

If you veer from these essential steps, your game of 'Coffee Chicken' goes awry and you miss your train, well, that's very silly of you and you only have yourself to blame.

What to do When People Start Talking Over You

There's a catalogue of awkwardness surrounding Going to See Things On Your Own, but for now we're going to focus on one very particular thing that could happen at the theatre or cinema: in the short time before a show or film is about to start, or in the interval, the two people sitting either side of you realise they know each other and start chatting.

What do you do if the lady to your right leans forward and starts speaking to the guy on your left, and they start free-flowing about how funny it is to run into him here of all places, and she wasn't going to say anything but then she just thought, well, might as well say hello, what does she have to lose? and you're stuck in the middle, while the conversation bounces over your head.

This is our five-point plan of action:

1 Look from one to the other, smiling, chuckling a little, as though part of the moment.

2 Hide: draw your programme/phone up very
   near your face.
3 Offer to swap seats with one of them.
4 Leave your seat: go to the loo or get popcorn.
5 Make a loud phone call so they can't hear each
   other.

We hope you'll go for a combination of 1 and 2
at first, until it becomes unbearable. If it's dragging
on and neither party has acknowledged you there in
the middle (very rude, but people are, you know),
then go for number 3. If they're still not full of

apologies at this point, you have our permission to go with number 4, or if you're feeling brave and a bit vengeful, number 5.

How do you Tell People Talking in Cinemas to be Quiet?

People talking in the cinema ranks very highly on the chart of middle-class irritations. It's now almost impossible to enjoy a whole film without kids and adults talking, sniggering, even making quite loud observations as though talking directly to the characters on screen. The middle-class person feels an urge and a duty to tell these people to be quiet, but it's difficult to know quite how to go about it. Here are a few suggestions:

1 The mid-distance 'shush'. This is nice and indirect, and often other middle-class people will join in and intimidate.

2 Slip out of the theatre and go and tell on them. It's the usher's job. To make sure it doesn't look like this is what you've been doing, pick up a bag of M&Ms on the way back through.

3 If feeling brave enough to tell them directly to 'please stop talking' (never 'shut up'), it's better for the woman to do it, unless the man is willing to front out a fight.

What to do When the Person Serving you in a Shop Talks on Their Phone

This retail experience is annoying and yet, sadly, increasingly common. Rather than ignore the ringing of their mobile, shop staff now seem perfectly content to pick up and answer it, and even chat throughout

the process of ringing up your goods. It seems alien to a middle-class person that someone can deal with you without giving you their full attention. To find them giving you no attention at all is thoroughly unpleasant.

On no account should you put up with this without a fight. It's not acceptable. The way to handle it is to keep eye contact with them and ask them lots of questions. 'Could I have another bag, please?' 'Could you check the price of this for me?' 'Are these apples locally sourced?'. Just keep dropping the questions in until they are forced to hang up on their call.

Of course, it cuts both ways, and you should never, ever answer your own phone if it rings while you're being served.

CHAPTER 8

A Guide to Middle-Class Relationships and Socialising

Here's where things get very tricky. It's hard enough being a middle-class person on your own at home or at work, but introduce partners, friends, parents and children into the mix and your life becomes a string of quandaries and awkward moments punctuated only by cringing and overanalysis. How on earth do you get people to leave when they've been hanging around too long after your dinner party? Why is everyone suddenly sending 'Save The Date' emails? Why is it important to bond over the coffee machine when you visit a friend's house? What is really going on when your other half says 'nothing' is the matter? In this chapter, we'll get to the heart of middle-class relationships, providing tips on how to survive and even possibly, thrive in your social circle.

Talking About Other Couples

Spending the weekend with friends is an essential middle-class ritual, which, like all essential middle-class rituals, is fraught with unspoken tensions. How drunk do you get on Saturday night? What will the two partners who only know each other because of the friendship of their spouses to talk about? How to get around the awkwardness when one couple's child discipline is stricter than the other's?

By the end of these weekends of activities, elaborate cooked breakfasts and photograph-album sharing, both couples can often feel exhausted and even desperate to escape. Which is why, perhaps, the god of weekend visiting made sure the best bit comes at the end.

We refer of course to the return-journey review, the post-match analysis in which the visiting couple mend tensions that may have opened up between them ('Did you have to tell him about my infection?') by discussing and agreeing about things they have noticed about the couple they were staying with. The odd new sofa of which they were so proud ('I thought it was awful, didn't you?'). The violent TV programmes they let the kids watch ('No wonder

they're so aggressive!'). And the enviable new kitchen ('Really lovely; that's how I'd like ours. I thought they were supposed to be skint, though?').

The return-journey review isn't necessarily mean. It can overflow with love and kindness just as it can brim with complaints and wry chuckles, and it's usually more about interest in the other couple than bitching or competition. In a way, it's like the discussions of characters you had in English lessons at school, although generally more interesting. Get started with our little list of promising return-journey review topics.

1 *Relationship:* who wears the trousers? Or, who seems not to wear the trousers but actually does, in subtle ways?

2 *Alcohol:* if they drink more than you, they may have a drink problem. Less, and they have become dreadful killjoys in their old age.

3 *Money:* awkward. Insistence on poverty instantly distrusted and prompts richer couple to list poorer couple's intangible advantages ('He can borrow his dad's vans any time he likes!').

4 *Children:* similar to alcohol. If their kids are disciplined

more strongly than yours, the parents are too uptight. Less strongly? Headed for trouble.

5 *Secrets:* the bit when she let slip the story about his stag night! Brilliant! You have to love them really, don't you?

Put an End to the Misery of STDs

You've surely noticed the increase in STDs: people sending out 'Save The Date' emails for events they're planning way in advance? If you're lucky enough to be unfamiliar with them, 'Save The Dates' are messages telling you that the sender is planning a party/charity event/whatever in several months and although they haven't sorted invitations yet, they want you to put the date into your diary now.

The problem is obvious. Without a STD, when confronted with an event you don't want to go to you can simply lie and say you are busy. If you responded

From: Miles
Subject: 18 June - save the date for Sarah's big vintage 4-0
Date: 2 Feb 2012 10:22
To: Jess

Please save Saturday 10 June in your diary.

It's Sarah's 40th!
I'm throwing a 1940s-themed party for her.

Formal invitation to follow.

Miles

to a STD a few months ago, you're tied into the event and there's really no way out if a better offer has come up, or if you have just decided you don't want to go. The whole thing is horrendous. On no account inflict a STD on someone else. The absolute worst thing you can do is spread this misery.

The Importance of Discussing Coffee-Makers

The first visit to a new friend's home is always a nervous occasion for the middle-class person. Will you be able to think of enough to talk about? Will you spill or scratch something? And, horror of horrors, will they be such accomplished hosts that you will be intimidated by the idea of inviting them back? Of course, there are upsides; the promise of an intimate friendship, interesting conversation – and the chance to see what their house is like.

The nerves are often supercharged around this latter point, so that the potentially awkward period of conversation after the initial greeting, coat-taking and direction-indicating can often be dealt with by the fixing of attention on the host's kitchen (which is usually where you will be at this point). Or, even better, the detailed discussion of a conspicuous design feature or gadget ('I really like how you've painted that wall', 'Is that a bottle opener? Wow – I see!').

The gadget chosen for discussion should not be too big or too fundamental to the house (e.g. the cooker), as that can seem a little covetous, nor should it be too small (e.g. novelty egg timer) to make extended conversation seem forced. Ideally it should be smallish, but one of many different variants, so that it is reasonable to have a long, slightly arch, discussion of its features.

All this means that the current number-one status gadget (having edged out, we would argue, the barbecue) is without doubt the coffee-maker. We advise that for the ideal social icebreaker, you natter about the Neff and coffee-making in general for at least twenty minutes.

How to Encourage Guests to Leave

There are those who always think they are in the way or outstaying their welcome and then there are those who presume your desire for their company is endless and your coffee machine is always brewing a fresh pot.

So how do you encourage the oblivious guest, feet up on the sofa, blathering away, to realise that it's time to make a move? First, it depends on whether you know that this is a habit of theirs. When you invite them, say you need to be up early the next

day or be somewhere later in the afternoon. You can then be quite blunt when it comes to it: 'Right, be off with you, I've got to go to bed/get ready for that thing.'

If you're caught out by a lingering guest or group of guests you don't know that well, the trick is to disrupt the atmosphere. The most effective way is to stand up and hover. Once you've stood up, whatever you do don't sit down again. Lean in a doorframe, against a mantelpiece – whatever, just stay standing. Eventually they'll have no choice but to stand up too. And leave. Taxi!

The Corner Seat: Always the Very Worst Place to Sit at Any Dinner Party

There is a distinct flaw in the way modern dinner parties are organised. One of the corners at the end of one side of a long rectangular table is almost always a bum deal that is highly restrictive to conversational options. The underlying problem is that the most popular shape of dining table is long and rectangular, and the usual number of people eating is eight or ten. After a few glasses of wine, one end of the table can't hear the other comfortably, and so, by the time the main course arrives, the conversation inevitably splits.

At this point, the person seated uptable of you is likely to join in the banter in the middle, leaving three of you at the end. You can't talk to the person opposite without appearing to ignore the other one at right angles to you at the head/foot and so in effect you are obliged to talk chiefly to this end-person, regardless of how much you have in common.

We can only suggest you be as pushy as you can bear when finding a seat. And if you do get stuck, you'll just have to attempt to break up the evening with prolonged trips to the loo.

Try the Handle or Knock? A Middle-Class Dilemma of Lavatorial Etiquette

The loo can be a source of much angst and uncertainty for middle-class people. Indeed, simply referring to it as a 'loo' was famously said by Nancy Mitford to disclose your social class. But there is a particular worry, which isn't often talked about.

It is this. Imagine you're at a house with people

other than your family – at a party, say – and you wish to use the loo. You find it – and the door is closed, with no indication of whether someone is inside or not. How do you find out if anyone's in there? Knock, or try the handle? Open the door gingerly and peer around? The potential horror of walking in and finding someone on the loo is just too much to contemplate. Knocking seems the polite thing to do but, if there is someone in there, it means you've acknowledged their presence and they feel compelled to say something – but what? There is no accepted message and so it's usually an awkward 'Only me!' or 'I'm in here!' or, even worse, the apologetic 'Won't be long!'. You have to reply ('That's fine!'), which sounds ridiculous, and means you are virtually in conversation with someone who, possibly, has their pants around their ankles. Aside from the awkwardness of that, it gets worse when they come out because they know the knocker was you.

The trying of the handle seems ruder, but it's good because it requires no conversation afterwards. When the person comes out, they don't know it was you who rattled. You can pretend to have bowled up that very second, while the ignorant, impatient handle-shaker has flounced off. It's the least embarrassing solution for all concerned.

Doing Everything in Fancy Dress

Twenty years ago fancy-dress parties were unusual, and people wearing fancy dress to events such as sports matches, or sponsored walks, were rare. These days it seems almost obligatory for any self-respecting middle-class person – perhaps more for men than for women – to wear fancy dress at least twice a year. Shops and web-based hire companies proliferate. Why?

It must have something to do with the modern taste for creating special occasions. The little gathering at home got chucked out with the chintz years ago, and these days no occasion (passing driving test, thirtieth birthday, coming home from hospital) is too minor for a mass surprise party with banners and a friend who 'can DJ a bit'.

But, despite our desperate desire to party and be loose and open like the Italians or the Aussies or whoever, most of us still struggle to shake off the British stiffness until we've had a drink. Fancy dress might be

the answer. Dressing like a cartoon character or the King of Pop helps with our stiffness a bit. Sometimes, that mad-scientist or handsome-prince mask is really saying, 'I am British and middle class, and if I could have one wish it would be to be someone else – until I've had a couple of Sauvignon Blancs, anyway.'

Going to All-Seater Gigs

All-seater gigs could be the perfect solution for the middle classes, who want to go to gigs but who get a bit uptight when our personal space is invaded, or when people push in and throw beer over our new Converse. Why should this be so? Five reasons:

1 No one expects you to dance, so you don't have to worry about whether you are too old for that sort of thing.

2 Everyone is sitting down, so you can actually see, which matters because these days you really like to appreciate the music.

3 The seats are allocated when you buy your ticket, so there is no pushing in.

4 You don't need to worry about where to put your coat.

5 No one stands on your feet, thereby damaging the seams on your shoes (see above).

The Prom Problem

It's no surprise that kids raised in a world where there is a McDonald's on every high street and a twenty-four-hour Disney Channel should have American dreams. But middle-class parents are facing the consequences full in the face: the end-of-year prom. Just the word makes us squirm.

In our day we might have celebrated finishing our O levels by watching *Blue Peter* without feeling guilty about revision. Or, if we were really lucky, a party with some contraband cider where someone might be sick in a bush. Whatever it was, it was low-key and British. We didn't make a fuss.

Today's GCSE girls demand big dresses and hair and make-up and accessories. They want prom dates. Worst of all, they want to arrive in a limo. Those awful stretch jobs beloved of tacky hen parties and Jordan-esque celebrities.

'But Daddy can drop you off in the Volvo' is met with derision.

And we're torn. Of course we want to reward them for all their hard work. We love to see them have fun with their friends. We're happy for them to celebrate. We just wish they would do it quietly.

The Modern Wedding List

Wedding lists are a source of tremendous anguish for a middle-class person. They create endless dilemmas and possibilities for bickering with your partner. Chances are, at least one of you doesn't even want to go to the wedding in the first place. By the time you look at the wedding list, you've probably already calculated how much you'll spend on travelling, hotels, new outfits ('Did I wear that dress to the last wedding, or was that the christening?'), kennel fees and bribes to persuade the kids to go with you without too much sulking.

You don't want to make your purchase too early: it'll look obvious that you were making sure the 'under £50' gifts hadn't all been snapped up. But leave it too late and, well, you know the risk.

As if it wasn't stressful enough, the wedding list's

162

gone mad in recent years. Nowadays we're invited to contribute to a couple's honeymoon, purchasing romantic meals in restaurants, boat trips and sight-seeing tours, not to mention £10 contributions to bottled water, pizza slices and other snacks that will be required as the couple walked around in the heat. Rumour has it that this sort of wedding list can even go as far as asking you to make £5 contributions to a new bed that the couple will need on their return. Too much info, perhaps, but think of it this way: at least it feels like you're contributing to something happy and kind of romantic rather than a piece of kitchen equipment that you just know will never see the light of day.

Greetings Cards

Until recently, the Easter card was an unusual, even eccentric thing to send or receive in Britain. The selection would be limited to one or two, probably stuffed in the recently cleared Mother's Day section, and generally they would be purchased by older churchgoing ladies to send to other older churchgoing ladies.

No longer, of course; all card shops now put up garish chick- and egg-strewn displays in early March, and in early April middle-class people throughout the land can be heard exclaiming, 'Oh, no! Chris and Annabel have sent us a bloody Easter card; I didn't know they sent them! Have we got one we can send in return?'

This is but one aspect of the modern middle-class phenomenon of obsessive greetings-card sending. Middle-class people – it is more often, but by no means exclusively, women – are sending greetings cards not merely for birthdays, Christmas and special occasions, but for almost any occasion that involves leaving the house. They send cute little cards with retro images saying, 'Was just thinking of you – hope you're feeling better!' And it has been known for them to send a card to thank someone for sending a thank-you card when one wasn't really needed.

Greetings cards have become like foil-wrapped chocolate mints – things that once signified luxury but are becoming so commonplace as to be consumed at least once a month. Although one shouldn't sneer. The middle classes lead lives that increasingly leave them feeling isolated and cut off from their real friends and from people who are kind to them; the desire to make contact and keep in touch must drive some of this, just as it drives some social networking. Our advice is to keep plenty of Easter cards in stock – although all good middle-class readers will already do this, of course.

Dealing with Embarrassingly Un-PC Parents

All middle-class people get secretly nervous when they have to introduce their parents to friends for the first time, for two reasons.

First, the middle-class person has usually left home and their comfortable but slightly weird childhood behind and created for public consumption a new, airbrushed version of their past that makes them seem more interesting and less swotty. (Of course, since everyone they know has done the same thing, everyone is aware their friends were a bit less interesting and more swotty than they make out, so this is one of those pointless quirks of middle-class behaviour, but anyway.) Parents can destroy this illusion with one innocently revealing memory: 'Do you remember crying when you came second in the

under-eighteens violin competition, dear?' 'How you fussed over being Prom Queen!' 'It did you the world of good, joining the Young Conservatives!'

Second, there is the problem of the parents themselves. For the snootier offspring, this may include parental taste; cringing when Dad expresses a preference for salad cream rather than mayonnaise, for example, or trying to keep the conversation off Mother's Botox treatments. But even if the middle-class person can laugh that off, there is the remaining problem of illiberal politics. All middle-class parents have embarrassing political views: if they're relaxed about immigration, they're uptight about 'the gays'. If they're tolerant on race and religion, they're right off with regard to the working classes or obsessed with being banned from saying certain words ('Are we allowed to call them gypsies nowadays?'). There is no escape; even trendy older liberals can reduce a dinner party to awkward silence with overenthusiastic celebrations of 'African sensuality' or similar.

It's all OK, though, because being middle class, the embarrassed person's friends will always rally round and, except perhaps in very extreme cases, make excuses for the parent. They don't necessarily believe these excuses, of course. They're just feeling a rush of happy gratitude that this time it wasn't their mum and dad acting like Nazis.

Five excuses you can make for other people's un-PC parents:

1 'It's just their generation.'
2 'From their point of view, perhaps they have a point.'
3 'I admire them for saying what they think.'
4 'My mum and dad are exactly the same; it's their age.'
5 'What? I never heard them say that.' (A lie, for particularly bad occasions.)

Chapter 9

How to Spend

The middle classes are very anxious consumers. We are convinced that what we buy, and where we buy it, not only reflects who we are but can change who we are, make us better people. We are defined by our stuff. This makes us exceedingly vulnerable in the face of marketing wheezes. It makes us want to talk at great length with our friends about the brand of buggy we've chosen – we can't bear for this sort of important consumer choice to go unnoticed. But it's not just the big-ticket items that can make or break our sense of self. Why is it that Percy Pigs make us feel so much better about life? How come we can bring ourselves to shop in Iceland but refuse to sign up for a Bonus Card? Let's start by exploring a very special middle-class relationship.

The Middle Classes and Marks & Spencer: A Special Relationship

The essence of the middle-class relationship with M&S is the tacit understanding it somehow communicates to you as you walk round one of its branches. It knows you need to feel special about the sweets that you give to your kids, so you get the Percy Pig range and that retro seventies packaging. It knows you don't want to think of yourself as lazy, so it keeps the ready-made sandwich fillings in inconspicuous places. And best of all, it knows that we know that it knows that most people use its shops for food and pants, so their Simply Food stores stock underwear and socks as a sideline, with no apologies. If you want a Swiss roll and a pair of knickers (and who doesn't?), then fine; all food shops should do this, but only M&S has the bottle. They should rebrand as Simply Food and Underwear, or Simply Snacks and Socks.

If M&S was ever to close down, maybe none of us would actually miss any of its products; you can buy that kind of produce anywhere nowadays. It's more likely that in these uncertain times, we just like the reassurance of knowing that it's there, like *Antiques Roadshow* and BBC costume dramas on a Sunday evening.

The Need-to-Know Buggy Brands

Modern middle-class men are a bit more easy-going and touchy-feely with their kids than they used to be. Once, blokes wouldn't be seen dead, in their local area at least, pushing prams or playing with their offspring, but now that sort of thing is almost a status symbol.

In conversations with men who are new dads, the chat often switches to the buggy. Twenty years ago, men took only a minimal interest in what model of Maclaren or similar their partner chose, but things have changed with the arrival of what is commonly referred to as 'the designer buggy', the rather showily designed four-by-four-style monster that retails north of three hundred quid. Because these are quite close to cars, men feel OK discussing them at some length, and in new-parent circles it is not uncommon to hear, slipped between a discussion of how embarrassing NCT classes are and how much their baby seems to like house music, a long debate about the relative merits of, say, Stokke, Britax and Bugaboo.

The discussions are usually carried out in just slightly arch voices, the God-I-can't-believe-we're-talking-about-this tone that new dads often affect to deal with the fact that, well, they can't believe they're talking about being a father. Non-parents will often feel excluded because, oddly, the rudeness rules that should forbid talking about stuff that excludes people get relaxed by many young parents. For those who wish to join in, however, here's a quick guide to the brands that might get mentioned, and some ideas of what to say.

Bugaboo

This is the chunky, very four-by-four-ish brand that is synonymous with the designer-buggy phenomenon. Many dads are faintly embarrassed by owning one, as they're such a cliché. The key is to discuss models (Cameleon (sic), Frog, Bee), and especially the new double buggy, the Donkey. Which, by the way, retails for £1,200.

Phil & Teds

Trendy, smart and adaptable for one or two kids, this is the buggy of choice for stylish young urban parents who are trying very hard to keep up a neat and chic outward appearance, despite their home probably being in total chaos. They feel much better about life once they're out and about pushing their Vibe, Verve or Promenade. Best to comment on the elegant contours of the sun canopy.

Stokke Xplory

This is the one – in case you've noticed – with the kid-basket bit at the pusher's chest level. The radical design tends to appeal to sporty men because it resembles golf equipment; they like it because they can see their little fella up close, and communicate better.

Maclaren

Generally much cheaper than the designer buggies, so the owner can play it one of two ways: be a bit embarrassed at having such a low-rent item, or go on the offensive and say you couldn't be bothered with all the fancy stuff. The latter can cause an awkward silence. If it's the Cath Kidston model, he'll probably try to stay as quiet as possible.

Quinny

Quite maverick; look strange, have three wheels and the individual models have whacky names such as

Buzz and Zapp. Not all that popular; fans tend to think of themselves as original thinkers, and very practical. Ask about how small they are when folded up – the major selling point of the Zapp.

iCandy

A less conspicuous choice than some of the other superbuggies here, but they nevertheless usually have interesting designs, especially in models catering for two children. Popular with people who claim they couldn't be bothered looking for long. Try expressing admiration for the large amount of luggage space at the bottom.

Trickle-Up: When we Need the Masses to Show us the Way

Sooner or later, if you're a coffee-drinker, you will have to consider an Nespresso machine. You may also know that if you are a coffee snob you will at first reject Nespresso because you assume Nestlé coffee must be crap, and then read on the internet that The Fat Duck serves Nespresso, and note that Amazon has about a billion positive reviews. You then realise that many of your coffee-snob friends have them, and get quite confused as you reassess a brand that middle-class liberals like you instinctively hate as much as McDonald's.

There is a little brand phenomenon going on here. We middle classes like to think that we set the trends, and are among the first people to adopt stuff that later trickles down to the masses. But there are some brands that started off as mass-market, only to be adopted by us and denied their original roots. This is the trickle-up top five:

1   Nespresso
2   Lidl
3   IKEA
4   Aldi
5   *The X Factor*

Loyalty-Card Denial

'Do you have a Bonus Card? Would you like one?'

A simple question, and yet one fraught with implications that chip at the very fabric of who we are. Data-protection issues? In-a-hurry issues? No. This is Iceland. You're shopping in an 'economy' supermarket on a short-term basis while it's still part of the recessionista downshifting trend, but still in denial about any longer-term loyalty issues. An Iceland Bonus Card would sit awkwardly in your wallet next to loyalty cards for Space NK, Village Books and the local non-chain café.

You're more than happy to take advantage of Iceland's cheap branded goods with their easy-to-add-up pricing strategy of everything seemingly rounded to the nearest pound. You get disproportionately excited over its high number of nostalgia brands like Bird's Custard Powder and Tunnock's Teacakes. And on several occasions you've bumped into people eyeing up the Special K who you know send their children to independent schools or who work for the BBC. But a loyalty card? Hmmm.

As we all know, loyalty cards mark you out as belonging to a tribe. They make a statement about your lifestyle values, or how you'd like your lifestyle to be perceived. A bit like buying posh jam even though you actually prefer the cheaper one because it's less lumpy, or following someone cerebral on Twitter.

While it is currently fashionable to mention your Asda online deliveries at drinks parties, or tweet your excitement that Aldi are selling tennis rackets this week, for most of the middle classes it is still a short-term adventure, Blitz spirit and all that. Something they assume they can drop as soon as this whole recession thing blows over and they can start booking Ocado daytime slots again (not just those secret Tesco deliveries after dark). It's rather like admiring the clean lines of a classic concrete estate knowing you'll never actually have to live there.

Worrying About Brands Being 'Too Middle Class'

When you hear people berating Radio 4 for being 'so f***ing middle class', you can't help objecting. Surely, you think, that's the whole point of Radio 4? Isn't it similar to complaining about, say, darts being too working class? We can't really see how Radio 4 could be very different without being something else entirely.

What is so terribly wrong with being middle class? MC products and services are something at

One organic
John Lewis
cotton bag

which the British excel, and we should start celebrating it, taking in this top five:

1 John Lewis
2 Radio 4
3 The National Trust
4 Jack Wills
5 Bottle Green

And while we're at it, let's reflect on all the things that would have been better if they had been *more* middle class, instead of trying to be 'street' or 'contemporary':

1 The bloody Olympics
2 Range Rover
3 The Savoy
4 Sainsbury's
5 Barbour

Avoiding Own-Brand Electrical Goods

The lower rungs of the electronics ladder are occupied by the likes of Alba and, most of all, Dixon's own brand, Matsui. Younger readers may not remember that before Currys and Dixons merged, their own brands were Saisho and Logic; after the merger, it became Matsui. Aspirational middle-class people haven't been able to stop themselves being snobby about Matsui, even if it is all made in the same factory (as one's penny-pinching parents always insisted). It always seemed like a crappy compromise that lacked the style of Sony, or Panasonic. And so today, with more fluidity in the market and brand allegiances, one rarely sees a middle-class home with much Matsui, unless it's a cheap second telly in the kitchen. If you're looking for a line in the sand between the middle class and working classes, we suggest this might be it: Samsung might have crossed over, but Matsui remains marooned.

Feedback-Form Fatigue

In days of yore, you could have a great meal, leave a generous tip and thank the staff profusely on exiting, and that was an end to it. But today? No such luck. You'll get an email the following morning thanking you for dining at the restaurant and asking for your thoughts on the experience. *Please take two minutes to give us your feedback*, it pleads.

The MCs don't want to grumble, but this all seems a bit much. What could they need to know that you hadn't communicated with the tip? And it also seems part of the modern tendency to request feedback for even the most mundane of daily encounters. *Every time* you call your bank, an automated someone on the phone tree asks if you'd be 'willing to complete a short survey' (you never are). At your daughter's school's open evening, there is a whole desk for suggestions you might have for improving the school environment.

If you do bother to fill them in, it never feels as if your complaints or suggestions are even remotely acted upon. And does any of it really take 'two minutes of your time'? Of course not.

Take a stand against it, and make the point by setting up your own survey service so that you can ask people to feed back to you on the quality and delivery of your feedback to them. It might not help you improve your feeding back, but it will at least make it appear that you care, which in the end is the whole point, we suspect.

Chapter 10

Middle-Class Motoring

The road is a scary place for the middle classes. Whether in the driving seat or hovering on the pavement waiting to cross, the middle classes in transit come up against all kinds of predicaments. What is it about roof boxes that makes us quite so resentful about life in general? Is there a middle-class way to handle the motorway service station? What do you communicate about yourself by sitting in a particular place in the car with other people? It's a mean old place, the road, and you'd do well to follow our guide to navigating it with middle-class flair.

The Car Roof Box: Today's Ball and Chain for The Middle-Class Motorist

Car roof boxes. Those aerodynamic grey plastic things that look like a cross between a boat and a tombstone, and which sit atop millions of once quite attractive motors as they traverse our nation between staycations

and days out. It's partly their ugliness that makes us hate them, but there's something else too. The fact that they exist now when they didn't exist before when we had larger families means that they speak of the massive clutter of stuff that we accumulate. All the extra pairs of shoes we don't need, the gadgets we won't use, the just-in-case things that we use once and then stuff into the cupboard under the stairs before offloading them at the school Christmas fair. We seem to do this in spite of ourselves.

We desperately want to live lighter and less en-cumbered, but somehow consumerism has got the better of us, and – because this is how it works – is forcing us into buying *another* bit of stuff so that we can move the original stuff around, like gluttonous and obese snails buying a new shell. We see no end to it. Doubtless we will need to buy tools to enable us to fix it on and then perhaps a bigger box next year.

How to be Middle Class at a Zebra Crossing

As a pedestrian at a zebra crossing, the will-they-or-won't-they-stop dilemma seems to have spawned a new habit among some. The more over-polite middle class among us vaguely raise a hand or arm in a gesture of thanks. Sometimes we'll nod, and mouth 'thanks', but generally it ends up being a strange gesture, almost as if we're raising a hand to karate-chop the vehicle's bonnet.

As well as a trend for thanking/acknowledging a driver for stopping, some of us have started making a point of hurrying over the crossing as quickly as we can. In many cases, we might even run, or at least adopt that self-conscious half-run, half-walk thing which seems to be an involuntary movement. It's as though we feel we should be apologising not only for making a driver stop, but for needing to cross the road in the first place.

The definitive middle-class way to cross is to hurry, often running, as described above. This ensures that you are not inconveniencing drivers and demonstrates how considerate you are. It's part of that pattern whereby the people at the extreme ends of the social spectrum seem unconcerned by other people's welfare. The wealthy will step out onto the crossing without even considering whether or not the traffic will stop. They will simply assume that it will. They won't alter the speed at which

they were walking and won't even notice the cars that have stopped for them. It comes across as an example of how the powerful and wealthy assume without thinking that what they want to happen, will happen.

At the other end of the spectrum, many working-class people will slow down and take their time to cause the maximum irritation. They will perform that affected side-to-side saunter/swagger and their mate will, of course, be cycling across but will not be holding onto the handlebars.

All the while, those of us in the middle will fret about doing the right thing. And we should carry on just as we are. After all, if we were all a little bit more considerate, like us, wouldn't the world be a nicer place?

Where to Sit in a Car When Travelling With Other People

Where a couple chooses to sit in a car when sharing said car with another couple is a sure guide to their social class. Take two couples, Couple A and Couple B. They are about to go somewhere in a car driven

by Husband A. If they are working class, Husband A and Husband B sit in the front, wives A and B get in the back, thus:

> Husband B   Husband A
> Wife A   Wife B

If they are middle class, the couples separate, thus:

> Wife A   Husband A
> Husband B   Wife B

And finally, the debauched upper class splits the couples:

Wife B	Husband A
Wife A	Husband B

Not grounded in academic research or anything like that, but interesting, isn't it?

How to be Middle Class at a Motorway Service Station

Middle-class Dad treats the motorway service station like a cross between a Formula One pit stop and an Ebola colony.

Knowing that he is about to experience something truly horrible, traumatic and shockingly common, he approaches the petrol forecourt at speed, warning wife and kids to get ready, taking any last-minute orders for Haribo, Evian and so on from the back seats. MC Dad homes in on a vacant pump and even if it's on the wrong side for his vehicle's cap he takes it, stretching the pipe over the car roof if required. As he fills, wife and kids make a dash for the loos.

Filled up, Dad runs, actually *runs*, up to the till. (He also wants to go to the loo but would rather hold it in until Petworth than have to go into one of those horrific communal lavatories that stink of wee and perfumed bleach.) As he queues, he grabs a bag of extortionately priced sweets and some water (totting up exactly how much less this stuff would cost anywhere else – and no, of *course* he doesn't have a sodding loyalty card) and then runs back to the car. If things have gone according to plan, wife and kids are now buckled up again. Even the shiny new middle-class-targeting Waitrose and M&S franchises haven't tempted them.

Back on the motorway again, the whole visit should have taken less than five minutes.

How to Drive a Soft Top Without Looking Ridiculous

Convertible ownership is a tricky area for the middle classes. It traditionally feels a little too shouty and flashy for the statement-averse professional. To drive with your hood down on those treasured blue sky days is the social equivalent of loudly guffawing in a quiet restaurant while swilling down vintage champagne and perhaps even slamming your fist on the table just to rub it in. Having an overtly good time in this way hasn't always been encouraged within middle class life. To show positivity towards an expensive item of such evident impracticality (we are, after all, inhabitants of an inclement island in the North Sea), and which so overtly prioritises feel-good over function, is instinctively troubling. But the increasing importance and value of life experience both for ourselves and our wider circle give convertibles a powerful counter argument: 'The dog can sit up front with me'; 'We'll use Dad's car for IKEA'. Memories – and framed photo murals outside the downstairs loo – are made of this.

Just mind you watch a few important dos and don'ts.

DO be prepared to drive with the hood down in changeable weather. The occasional damp and wind-swept journey is both agreeably eccentric and eliminates any perception of smugness from your hardtop driving fellow road users.

DON'T hurry to fix any dents or imperfections on your hood or bodywork. A malfunctioning electric hood that requires additional manual force each time you use it is merely karmic payback for that blissful weekend you spent in Dorset last September.

DO bemoan its impracticality and silliness whenever

it crops up in conversation. The positives are implied in your cheerful castigation and are palpable to anyone listening.

DON'T be tempted with going long on the stereo volume in traffic or town. It may feel like the perfect chance to crank up the Neil Young but it'll sound better without the self-conscious discomfort once you hit the B roads.

DO litter the interior with top-down driving accessories that cement your car as less vehicle and more lifestyle: a crusty stick of melted sunblock, a baseball cap you

got free through work softball,
a cracked pair of aviators, a fleece
gilet that lives on the backseat.

DON'T call it a 'rag-top' if it's a metal folding roof –
in short, a little knowledge of open-top history goes a
long way. Do call it 'the car', never 'the convertible'.

DO drive in winter, but you'll need to balance the
merits of a fleeting sensory experience with the
environmental and financial factors of putting your
fan heaters on overdrive. Your call.

DO familiarise yourself with the soft top tribes on
the road – to help you know your place among
convertible drivers, follow our handy guide to the
top ten tribes.

Soft Top Tribe #1 – The Damn Wrights: the BMW 3 Series Convertible

Jez and Carol wouldn't swap their navy blue 320i
for anything – 'Sure, it's a few years old now but
guess what? The Germans know how to make a
bloody good car.' They got it with 8k on the clock
after Clarkson had given it five stars in *Ingear* – as
Carol says, you'd have to have a screw loose to buy

anything new – and it's been all the way down to Biarritz without a hitch, not counting those barmy French drivers, of course. Jez still wishes he'd trusted himself and hadn't let the satnav lead him on a goose/oie chase around the Bordeaux rocade.

Soft Top Tribe #2 – White Vain Man: the BMW Z4

Sometimes Jamie wonders if he should have gone for an Audi TT when he had that lump sum from the house sale knocking around but he's actually wanted one of these ever since he saw Pierce Brosnan drive the original version in *GoldenEye*. When a friend from university bought his wife one too, Jamie started looking online at a few alternatives, but when he's driving down the country lanes near his dad's house or just when he catches his reflection in a building in town – curvy lines, Titan Silver bodywork, aviators, white shirt, arm out the window – he know it's going to be hard to give up.

Soft Top Tribe#3 – Chaveau Riches: the MINI Roadster

Tash knows she's lucky to have her little MINI Roadster, but she's worked hard for it so why shouldn't she have a bit of a treat? It's her little home from home – she keeps her make-up in the front, her Tom Ford sunnies in the glove box and there's always a pair of heels (or three!) in the boot as you just never know. It can still make her smile from a distance when she sees the lovely shape of the canvas roof, the round headlamps and the private plates that Scott gave her on their anniversary weekend at The Grove.

Soft Top Tribe #4 – The Jack Pack: Audi A3

Mark's always wanted an A3 but wasn't mad keen on the convertible version at first – he was worried the boys might rib him about hairdressers, chavs and all that stuff. When he phoned Sophie from an auction (his cousin who does a bit of importing took him along) there was no going back. Her voice cracked a bit when she saw it and still describes it as 'a-mazing' to friends, though these days she doesn't really put the hood down at all as the wind doesn't agree with her new fringe.

Soft Top Tribe #5 – Saga Louts: Triumph Stag

Jenny rolls her eyes in faux disapproval when the Stag comes up in conversation with friends at dinner but it was her that encouraged Lionel to take the plunge as a retirement project, knowing it would keep him busy and no doubt give them a few funny stories along the way. 'She needs a bit of looking after,' Lionel will reply, 'but when she's firing it's all worth it… and the car's not bad either!' He takes it out on Monday mornings in his over-worn deck shoes which allow him to really feel the vibrations through the sole. 'Sure beats work,' he tells no one in particular when hanging the keys up back in the kitchen.

Soft Top Tribe #6 – Loft Wingers: Saab 900 convertible

'The Saab', as they both call it, is getting a bit long in the tooth now, quite throaty for long journeys and after a couple of hefty garage bills it gets a lot less use than in the old days. Tom tends to use his fixie for short trips but loves having what he regards as a genuine design classic sitting outside his door and has been known to just sit inside, using the Blaupunkt in-car system to catch up on some old mix tapes. Anna prefers it in the rain with the atmospheric patter on the canvas  hood, the squeaky wipers that still need fixing and an old Suzanne Vega album she picked up in the Pets in Need of Vets shop on the High Street.

Soft Top Tribe #7 – The Can Dos: VW Eos

Choosing the Eos really was a no-brainer. Sleek, well-designed and with a premium feel throughout, the clincher was knowing that it is purpose-built as a convertible not just an adaptation – all the learnings VW has gained as a carmaker channelled into one elegant and forward-looking four-seater. Even if they have had some trouble with the gearbox and Phil thinks the electric roof isn't as quick as it used to be, it still feels perfect for where their life is headed in the next 12–18 month period. Sue keeps a gratitude diary in the front for when she gets stuck in traffic on the way home.

Soft Top Tribe #8 – Jamie Oliver's Army: Renault mégane convertible

When Steph heard a friend of her mum's was selling, it seemed like the perfect interim car. A bit of good-value fun before Matt's freelancing picked up a bit and they could save some cash for a deposit on the MINI. Matt doesn't tell Steph quite how much he dislikes it but she can tell a lot from his face when the screaming four-cylinder engine hits 70, and he did tell her once at a birthday lunch that he thinks it's really aimed at old people. 'At the moment it's a Renault Mégane,' as Steph always says, 'but what we'd really like is…'.

Soft Top Tribe #9 – The Fun-Nancial Sector: Mazda MX-5

They first got the idea in the Lake District where they like to go walking every autumn – 'Why wait until we're old and grey?' said Jo. Rav didn't think it was the right time to mention he started to go grey four years ago. Their favourite thing about life in the MX-5 is that it brings out the best in other people too: when you're smiling, they're smiling. Life's about the simple things after all and any opportunity to get this point across shouldn't be missed.

Top Tribe #10 – Alt.middle: Volvo C30

David and Kate do not have a soft top. They can't help thinking the whole idea is absolutely cringe in England – even in California they look smug, so why would you have one in Chipstead? A colleague of David's from work had a convertible Golf GTI they all once squeezed into for a trip to the pub. It was fun in a silly 'take it or leave it' kind of way. Come to think of it, they don't see that couple much any more.

Chapter 11

Going on a
Middle-Class Holiday

For the middle-class holidaymaker, it is not a simple matter of getting from A to B and having a thoroughly nice time. There are all manner of snaggy moments to contend with. Is there a right way to handle the reclining seat on a plane – your own and the one in front of you? Is it OK to admit that you're actually really bored at sites of historical interest? And then there's the journey home and the holiday post-mortem. What's the etiquette around the holiday snaps and is there an art to bragging about your trip? In this chapter, we're all going on a middle-class holiday. So make sure you've booked your Speedy Boarding pass . . .

How to Master the Fine Art of Boasting About Your Summer Holiday

In years gone by, it was fairly straightforward and easy to show your status by the type of holiday you chose. In the eighties, a villa in the South of France or a cruise would show you had class and wealth. In the nineties a more luxurious beach holiday in the Maldives or a trip to Australia could make you the envy of your friends.

But since then, the world seems to have shrunk, and hitherto exclusive places have become much more accessible to the masses. Every Tom, Rick and Harriet has been to Australia; the Seychelles are as unattainable as Blackpool; and villas are standard. Blame the low-cost airlines, blame the internet, blame the adventurous spirit of people from Sheffield; whatever the reason, the fact is that it is harder than ever to impress anyone with your summer destination.

Of course, this doesn't stop people trying. And as we have been angling to score points against our friends and neighbours, so a new set of unspoken rules has been emerging – a kind of holiday brag version of paper, scissors, stone. It's hard to be exact and comprehensive about these rules, but a rough guide to the important ones follows. It might at least help you pass the time in your hot stuffy workplace while you count down the hours to that once-in-a-lifetime trek along the Inca trail.

A package holiday booked through any major travel agent loses to everything. If the package holiday is all-inclusive you are instantly disqualified, and will have to work hard to ever be admitted to a game of holiday brag again. However, see point 6.

1 Gîte beats villa (unless villa is owned by a celebrity).
2 Yacht beats gîte.
3 Camping holiday in Cornwall beats cottage in Devon.
4 But both are beaten by camping holiday in area of outstanding beauty in Wales, ideally one previously undiscovered until *you* found it.
5 Activity holiday (cycling, pony-trekking, mountain-climbing) beats beach holiday
6 Holiday anywhere beats your friend's holiday if they have taken their children out of school during term time. This applies to some, but not all, package holidays.
7 Holiday in New Zealand beats holiday in Australia. Australia beats South Africa. Touring Canada beats all, especially if it features trains and/or Alaska.
8 India beats Thailand. But not if your destination is Goa. If you book an all-inclusive to Goa, you might as well never come home again.

9   South America beats North America. This does not apply if your destination is Cancún, but if you lie and claim you are going to Tulum, you can fudge the issue.

10   Tunisia and Egypt beat Turkey, as they make you seem brave and interesting rather than merely tight.

The Easyjet 100m Dash

EasyJet is now a bona fide, MC-endorsed brand; fly to Ibiza or Majorca, Pisa or Genoa on EasyJet in the summer and the Bodenisation of the airline is immediately evident. As if to acknowledge its upwardly mobile image, a couple of years ago EasyJet launched its 'Speedy Boarding' initiative – and it worked well for a while, but it soon became clear that the programme had a serious flaw.

Yes, an extra tenner or so got you to the front of the queue in the departure lounge, but once you were on the bus it was every man for himself. EasyJet only cared about your privilege for so long. The doors hissed open and you had to make a dash for the aeroplane stairs, your prestige status evaporating as you dropped duty-free bottles of booze all over Luton's tarmac in your haste to get to the plane.

As the Speedy Boarding clan grew, an awkwardly segregated area in the aforementioned coach (a length of spring-loaded tape, basically) and a slightly staggered opening of the coach doors (i.e. Speedy Boarders off first) were introduced. But this didn't stop the ugly, rugger-like dash for the big orange steps once the bus began emptying. Speedy Boarding, briefly beloved of the slumming, vacationing middle classes, had lost its cachet.

But Verbier-bound skiers need not worry because EasyJet has invented, wait for it . . . SPEEDY BOARDING PLUS! 'Following feedback from customers, EasyJet has enhanced the Speedy Boarding product for those passengers who still need to check baggage into the hold of the aircraft by combining Speedy Boarding with a dedicated check-in service – Speedy Boarding Plus, offering a new level of customer experience which will be available at many airports across the airline's growing network,' the EasyJet website explains.

But here's the thing. Are Speedy Boarding and Speedy Boarding Plus really worth it? Yes, if you make a run for it you might get into row one, or bag an emergency-exit row with extra legroom, but after that – what exactly is the advantage?

Budget air travel is hell anyway. But it's often only an hour or two of hell and overpriced Mexican wraps and three-quid cups of coffee. If you are truly middle class, you won't get sucked in by such silly, snooty one-upmanship as Speedy Boarding. You're better off grinning and bearing it, politely queueing up and resolutely *not* being one of those braying types in chinos and a Ralph Lauren puffa who winds up all the Superdry lads reading *Nuts*. You don't want to be *that* kind of middle class.

Attempting to Portray Confidence in the Business Lounge

Middle-class people are prone to self-consciousness and introspection, but being in the presence of people lower down the social order gives us an external focus, i.e. behaving in ways that imply social superiority (this is partly why we MCs enjoy football matches so much).

Once surrounded exclusively by other MCs, we begin thinking about our manners and our relative status and it makes us twitchy; this is particularly true for those most competitive of middle-class males in the business community. The result is much avoiding of eye contact or, conversely, compensating with open-shouldered displays of confidence – spreading yourself out in those brooooad armchairs, or loudly comparing lounges you've visited around the world.

Here are our suggestions to ensure you show confidence in the Business Lounge:

- Loosen your tie, spread your limbs out on the armchairs and use an iPad.
- Rearrange the furniture to suit yourself.
- Take your time, and look nonchalant, when choosing and pouring drinks.
- Don't eat the nuts.
- Fall asleep.

The Reclining Seat:
A Mind and Body Endurance Challenge

For a traditional middle-class Briton travelling by air in economy class, a reclining aeroplane seat is fundamentally pointless, because our inherent awkwardness stops us

from reclining for fear of irritating the person behind. Rather than risk offending anyone, you spend ninety per cent of the journey locked in a battle of mind versus body: the former preventing you from ever feeling confident enough to recline, the latter complaining about its cramped legs. More troubling than that, though, is the situation where the person in front reclines his seat the moment the seatbelt light goes off. As the agonised MC traveller, you must of course say nothing. Consider it an important mind and body endurance challenge. You'll be a better middle-classer for it.

The Embarrassing Secret Boredom You Feel at Sites of Great Historical Interest

Say you've spent several days driving the hundreds of miles from Los Angeles to the Grand Canyon in Arizona. On arriving, you and your friend park up and walk to the edge to gaze out on this vast, natural wonder. Then you drive a little farther along, and gaze from a different angle. After about forty minutes, you have to acknowledge an uncomfortable fact: you've seen it, you thought it was incredibly spectacular, you were glad you came, and, er, that was quite enough, thanks. Feeling oddly guilty, you do what anyone would do in that situation – prolong the visit by going to the

gift shop and café. This is a familiar feeling for many middle-class people, who have journeyed to important sights or ruins and felt awkwardly underwhelmed. Being middle class, we feel obliged to hang around, but there is no need. Just take a picture and go back to the hotel. It's all anyone wants to do, really.

The Holiday Photograph

Back in the days when holidays tended to be a week on the Costa Packet and travelling was something you did to and from work, holiday photographs were

a bit of a joke. If a middle-class neighbour promised to pop round to talk you through their Bonusprints of Majorca, you hoped they were not the kind to linger on the details of every picture; the ones who invited you over to look at their slides became a standing joke. However, in our age of a) cheap and more adventurous travel, and b) digital photography and printing, the situation has been transformed.

The modern MC home is now not truly furnished without at least one large-framed print, probably hung in the hallway, taken on a family holiday to a non-European destination. The family may be in the picture or not, but the key difference between these displayed images and the old holiday snaps is that the background – the real subject – is more cultural than scenic. It may be of a bazaar, festival or camel market, or of striking and famous buildings; what it should not be of is a beach or a simple 'view'. The more interesting and unusual the picture, the better it serves as a conversation point, and the popular hallway positioning means that it often serves as a useful icebreaker with strangers visiting for the first time. In this sense, the new holiday snap could be seen as a badge displaying the family's taste to newcomers, but to see it serving solely as such would be cold and mistaken. Moments of relaxed family togetherness are not common these days, and the holiday photograph may serve as a daily reminder of one, and why you keep working so hard on this strange, grey and rather damp little island in the first place.

Suitable subjects for hallway holiday snaps

1 New York skyline
2 Moroccan souk
3 The summit of Mount Kinabalu
4 Indian festival
5 Animals in safari park
6 Mountains in Nepal
7 South African veldt
8 Barrier reef, taken from glass-bottom boat

Wearing a Dashiki and Jeans for the Journey Home

Pack. Taxi. Airport. Check-in. Fly. Land. Rain. Taxi. Home. Unpack. Why, wonders the middle-class traveller the day before setting off to go home, does the journey always go faster when you know you are in the office the next day? Perhaps the sheer volume of memos, emails and other assorted bits of paper waiting for you in your in-tray affects time itself. In any event, the journey home is just a sunburned, back-to-front, fast-forward version of the journey there. With added lethargy and misery.

The homeward leg does, however, have its own unique hurdles, which any middle-classer worth their salt must overcome. The first challenge – and one of the biggest – comes before the journey even begins. What to wear on the way? Wear what you've had on while away, and you'll look wrong once you land. Wear your domestic look while abroad, and you'll spoil the last few hours. What to do?

Ideally the middle-class person would arrive back in England in a full djellaba, proving that their cultural horizons have been broadened and of course that they got on rather splendidly with the locals. But there are practical considerations; traditional North African dress is fine in North Africa but doesn't fare too well in drizzly England. The best solution is to combine elements of cultural dress with practical travelling gear. Jeans with a madiba shirt, or a dashiki with a jumper underneath, will allow an arrival home in comfort and multicultural style.

Accent Acquirement: Stop It

There's always one, isn't there? One person who comes back from a trip to Disneyworld with just the slightest tinge of American about their accent, or a teeny lengthening of the vowel sounds. Of course they claim they 'don't realise' they're doing it, but no one is fooled and everyone thinks it's ridiculous: you spent ten days there, not ten years. And by the way, constantly repeating the insignificant bit of French or Spanish you learned isn't acceptable either.

CHAPTER 12

Have a Merry Middle-Class Christmas

We have made it to the most wonderful time of the year. And in many ways, that is actually true for the middle classes. Christmas time gives us permission to relax (a little bit) our worrying about tastefulness, and throw ourselves into the trashy merriment of it all. In this chapter, we reveal the Christmas guilty pleasures that are perfectly acceptable for the MCs to enjoy. But, of course, there are all sorts of awkward micro-moments at Christmas too – we can never quite escape them. So, whether Christmas starts for you on the first Sunday of Advent, or not until the *Radio Times* Christmas double issue comes out, use this chapter to identify and resolve the dilemmas that crop up during the festive season. Is there an ideal gift to buy for Secret Santa? What are the conversation topics you can fall back on when everything goes silent at the Christmas table? First, though, let's establish what type of MC festive celebrator you are, based on when the whole thing kicks off in your house . . .

The Christmas Countdown: When Does it Really Begin?

Different middle-class people have very defined, and very different, ideas about when Christmas gets under way. Below are the starting points for the main Christmas tribes; how do you start yours?

The 6th of November: The Maximalists

Really love Christmas, and get going once Bonfire Night's over and the ads begin in earnest. Decorations up on 1 December; cry when they're taken down.

The first Sunday of Advent: The Classicists

Genteel, churchy and likely to be older; begin writing Christmas cards when the first candle on the Advent crown is lit, but prefer restrained decoration and a small tree.

The 11th of December: The Personal Organisers

Buy tree a week after they go on sale because unable to rest until job is ticked off list. Spend two months trying to get organised in advance, but always fail.

The 18th of December-ish/Publication of the Radio Times *Christmas issue: The Christmas Specials*

Like to make the most of the season but don't like to spread it too thin. Prefer home-based festivities and big on nostalgia. Enjoy planning festive TV viewing.

The 20th of December-ish – last Friday before Christmas: the Office Party Posse

Probably under thirty. Don't think much about it until the works drink on the last Friday before breaking up. Spend final few days frantically buying gifts and likely dodging colleague they snogged at the drinks do.

The 23rd of December: The Minimalists

Favour perfunctory decoration
and celebration, consider most of it
commercial nonsense, apart from the
hearty walks.

The 25th of December: The Drinkers

Loathe the season, and put it off until last
minute by getting drunk on the 24th –
only to wake with a hangover that makes
it all seem even worse. Don't decorate
at all if they can help it.

Overreacting to Non-Issues in the Run-Up to Christmas

In middle-class circles, you hear the phrase 'it ruined
our Christmas' quite often. Nothing is too trivial
to cause ruination. It can be something as simple
as M&S selling out of your favourite party canapés
('Oh, but we have those every year!') or your being
unable to get the Ocado delivery slot you needed.

Or perhaps you buy your sister-in-law the same Cath Kidston item as someone else ('Oh, and I thought it was such an original gift!') or those beautiful table decorations didn't arrive on time and your carefully planned Christmas theme just won't be the same without them ('I ordered them in November, for Christ's sake! How could this have happened? It's all ruined now!').

We're all vulnerable to this hysteria really, and no wonder, with all the adverts and everything putting the pressure on. What we need to do is relax and take heart from the true meaning of the festival; after all, what would have happened if the Virgin Mary had been of the same mind? '*Full*? For crying out loud, Joseph, we might as well go back to Nazareth now! This mini-break is *ruined*!'

It's Father Christmas, Not Santa, Please

How outrageous that Father Christmas is fighting the North American character Santa Claus for rights to the British chimney. And it's not even Santa Claus any more, just Santa – a horrible diminution of historical characters into one brand-like entity. It's cringeworthy when a British person says it – adult or child, but especially adult, actually; we should know better. Father Christmas is an altogether lovelier name, and lovelier concept. The daddy of Christmas. The guardian of gift-giving. How can 'Santa' even compete with that? C. S. Lewis preferred Father Christmas for *The Lion, the Witch and the Wardrobe*. The illustrator Raymond Briggs preferred it for his graphic novel *Father Christmas*, which depicts the big man as a grumpy old git who's more interested in drink than presents. Ideal for British sensibilities! Apparently, in some spheres he's known as Kris Kringle, which sounds like a budget cereal. We'd be best off ignoring that one.

Respect, Please, Ladies and Gentlemen, for the Early Christmas-Card Sender

Just over a week into December, it's always interesting to tot up the number of your friends who were sufficiently organised to get their Christmas cards off in the first few days of Advent. It's certainly a question of mindset and manners; unlike crass multiple mail-out businesses who send in November, the early sender would never write or post before the start of December. One imagines them, a mass-ed rank of to-do list crossers-off with pens, cards, stamps and address books at the ready, barely able to wait until they can get going, get them off and then move on to the next job of putting up the decorations. Not present-buying, of course; that was completed in October. All we have to say is: hats off to you.

Equally Hard to Give as to Receive: the Not-so-Secret Anxiety of Secret Santa

At work, it has become commonplace to buy gifts for colleagues. This is yet another source of festive angst for the middle classes; should you buy presents for your colleagues? If so, which ones do you include and which ones do you leave out? How embarrassed will you be if you buy gifts but they don't buy you one in return? Or, worse still, if they buy you one but you have nothing to give them?

You would think that the Secret Santa option in the workplace would be an ideal solution to the problem. But no – Secret Santa brings with it a whole range of

snags both for the giver and the receiver of the gift. They can be summarised as follows:

Main worries for the giver (who is paranoid that everyone will realise their identity)

1 What if everyone else has bought more elaborate gifts and yours seems a bit tight?

2 What if everyone else has bought something small but meaningful but you've bought something far too elaborate?

3 What if everyone else has bought gifts that are

funny, quirky or really say something about the person? Your gift is boring and impersonal and shows your lack of imagination and understanding of your workmates.

4 What if you buy something that is too boring and you offend the receiver by implying that they are dull?

5 What if you buy something that is a little risqué and you offend the receiver by implying that they are common?

Main worries for the receiver (who has it relatively easy)

1 The gift you receive is boring and completely impersonal. You think this means that everyone in the office thinks that you are boring and have no interests.

2 The gift you receive is rude/suggestive in some way. You think this means that everyone in the office thinks you are brazen or vulgar.

3 The gift you receive is clearly meant to be personal to you, yet is something unpleasant. You think this means that everyone thinks you have bad taste.

4 You receive alcohol. Secretly you're quite pleased, but then you worry that everyone thinks you are so dull and insular that they just couldn't think of anything interesting to get you.

To assuage these fears, here are three things that will convey a neutral message:

- Fudge. But artisan, preferably. You don't want to say 'you like eating, so here's some average fudge', but rather 'you really appreciate fine foods, here's some quality fudge'.
- A scented candle. Go for a proper luxury one, though, not one that could be mistaken for an air-freshening device.
- Some sort of trendy kitchen accessory such as salad servers in bamboo or something.

Acceptable Christmas Guilty Pleasures

Christmas, we have decided, is about the relaxing of taste. For a few days, you can enjoy things that at other times of the year would seem a bit naff or not even particularly appealing. In some cases it's to do with nostalgia (you might even fancy a

sugared almond or a Meltis New Berry Fruit), but more often it's just a combination of indulgence and the Christmas spirit. Here are the top ten acceptable slightly trashy guilty pleasures:

1 Singing along to 'Stay Another Day' by East 17.
2 Listening to Classic FM as you cook Christmas dinner.
3 Drinking Dooley's Toffee Liqueur while watching DVDs. And Bailey's, of course, but that doesn't count, as relatively tasteful.
4 Tijuana Brass Christmas albums.
5 Quality Street. And Roses, if you're hardcore.
6 Tinsel. Not the modern, wide-cut variety, but thin, old-fashioned stuff. In red.
7 Paxo Sage and Onion stuffing for nostalgic reasons. Though families have been known to split up over less.

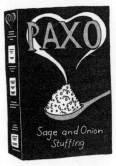

8 Giving yourself a day off from recycling everything, so it's easier to cook.

9 Watching *Home Alone* and other nineties children's classics. And *Jason and the Argonauts*, if you're male.

10 Staying in bed for most of Boxing Day morning, if necessary by feigning sleep.

The Law of Diminishing Fridge Returns

Isn't it lovely when the fridge is full of fresh festive food? The shopping's just been done and you're not allowed to touch any of the new stuff until whoever's in charge in your house declares the official start of Christmas. And once you've started, The Law of Diminishing Fridge Returns kicks in: over three days, you bring out the same foods – cold cuts, potato salad, pears in red wine – not quite finishing them up, storing them in smaller containers, bringing them out again at the next meal, trying to make them presentable and appetising, still not finishing them, and so on.

You spent time and money providing this bounty, damn it. It would be criminal to throw it away. But, quite honestly, by the 27th, you hate the sight of that potato salad. If anyone says 'cold cuts' one more

time, you won't be responsible for your actions. Your voice trembles with barely suppressed rage as you encourage your loved ones to 'please finish up the pears'. Come the 28th, everyone's gone home, the house is quiet and it's just between you and your fridge. Time to take the law into your own hands. You fire up the waste-disposal unit, send those leftovers to a grisly end – and gleefully get on the phone to order a pizza.

The Christmas Stress Goes on: What is the Last Posting Date for Festive Thank You Cards?

There are some activities that very simply distinguish the middle classes from other people – and one of them is the sending of thank you cards after receiving presents. And there is an angsty politeness that accompanies the ritual. Now your children's birthdays and Christmases are not complete without you sitting on the sidelines and noting down givers and gifts given so that you don't forget. Sending letters is a jolly nice thing to do, and we all feel terrible if we forget, but goodness, the stress that it can bring! Inevitably there are one or two gifts that have no tags – does one guess, or try to work out a tactful way of enquiring with the suspects? Is it OK to use 'Thank You' stationery, so it's quicker? And how long is it acceptable to take to reply?

Of course, more efficient friends have done theirs long ago, their promptness reminding you of the devastatingly impressive organisation of those supermums who get their child's post-birthday Thank Yous off within forty-eight hours of the party ending. You, though, will be doing the last batch at ten o'clock on Sunday evening in a perfect vignette of British middle-class life, i.e. secretly driving yourself mad with the effort of appearing perfectly calm and civilised. Right – did James and Charlotte send the Jellycat bear or the Usborne Snakes and Ladders?

The Back-to-Work Question: Did you Have a Good Christmas?

You'll definitely have been asked the great early-January question, 'Did you have a good Christmas?' before and expect to be asked many times more in the future. There are two points to note about this. One, how the word 'good' is slowly edging out 'nice' (American influence, we think) and two, how awkward it is to say that actually, your Christmas wasn't particularly good or nice. Unpleasant things often happen in the festive period – but with middle-class and professional people you tend to feel you'd be dragging the conversation down a bit if you said, 'No, my uncle died on Boxing Day.' The thing to remember is that the question is really just a 'hello' in disguise, and it doesn't warrant an actual answer. In fact, to give an actual answer is quite grotesque, and would show that you have no idea about middle-class social laws. Just as you should always answer the 'How are you?' question (also not a real question) with 'Very well, thanks' even if you are horrifically ill/heartbroken/bereaved/whatever, you should always, always reply to the Christmas question with 'Lovely, thank you', and then let everybody move swiftly on.

Credits and Acknowledgements

Editors:

Editor-in-Chief— Amy Hitchenor
Editor — Maddie York

Creative:

Art Director — David Rainbird
Creative Direction — Dan Holliday and Richard Benson
Illustration — Mia Nilsson

Project Management:

Sarah Henriques, Emma Thornton and Siobhan Sleet

Contributors:

Stephen Armstrong, Beth Bate, Guy Benson, Richard Benson, Kevin Braddock, Malika Browne, Jessica Cargill-Thompson, Hanna Charmers, Swiss Cottage Kev, Becky Davis, Will Hersey, Louise Jolly, Burt Kapur, Charlie

Layton, Jessica Mayne, Simon Mills, Sheila Speed, Spellman, Sharon Tanton, Billy Woods, Maddie York, Mike Daniels, Ben Newman, Nick Moss, Gillian Potkins, Theresa Wells, Frances Brown, Arthur English, Monty Verdi, Mark Harrison, Ruth Cox, Blonde M, Jessica Summerfield, Fanny Fandango, Simon Marsh, Issy Wells, Will Hogan

Special thanks to:

Richard Benson, Anwen Hooson, Laura Craik, Fraser Hardie, Martyn Evans, Dean Barratt, Jennifer Kabat, Yusuf Chuku, Shane Walter, Pete Lyle, Kenneth Hill, Anna Guyer, Julian Ball, Maria Williams, Gordon McMillan, Billy Woods, Alex Bilmes, Johnny Davies, David Godwin Associates, Charlotte Macdonald, Andreas Campomar, Elen Lewis, Steve Thompson, John York, Fiona York, Nicola Jacobs, Bea Roberts, Rosie Whitehead, Alex York, Luisa Kunstova, Ekow Eshun

Index

INDEX